D0020026

UCD WOMEN'S CENTER

Also by Barbara Ehrenreich

Dancing in the Streets: A History of Collective Joy

Bait and Switch: The (Futile) Pursuit of the American Dream

Nickel and Dimed: On (Not) Getting By in America

Blood Rites: Origins and History of the Passions of War

The Snarling Citizen

Kipper's Game

The Worst Years of Our Lives:
Irreverent Notes from a Decade of Greed

Fear of Falling: The Inner Life of the Middle Class

The Hearts of Men:
American Dreams and the Flight from Commitment

Global Woman:
Nannies, Maids, and Sex Workers in the New Economy
(WITH ARLIE RUSSELL HOCHSCHILD)

Re-making Love: The Feminization of Sex
(WITH ELIZABETH HESS AND GLORIA JACOBS)

For Her Own Good: 150 Years of the Experts' Advice to Women
(WITH DEIRDRE ENGLISH)

Witches, Midwives, and Nurses: A History of Women Healers
(WITH DEIRDRE ENGLISH)

Complaints and Disorders: The Sexual Politics of Sickness
(WITH DEIRDRE ENGLISH)

The Mean Season: The Attack on the Welfare State
(WITH FRED BLOCK, RICHARD A. CLOWARD,
AND FRANCES FOX PIVEN)

THIS
LAND
IS THEIR
LAND

Barbara Ehrenreich

THIS LAND IS THEIR LAND

Reports from a Divided Nation

A Holt Paperback

Metropolitan Books / Henry Holt and Company

New York

Holt Paperbacks
Henry Holt and Company, LLC
Publishers since 1866
175 Fifth Avenue
New York, New York 10010
www.henryholt.com

Library of Congress Cataloging-in-Publication Data

Ehrenreich, Barbara.
   This land is their land : reports from a divided nation /
Barbara Ehrenreich. — 1st ed.
      p.   cm.
   Includes index.
   ISBN-13: 978-0-8050-9015-4
   ISBN-10: 0-8050-9015-0
   1. Social problems–United States.   2. United States–Social conditions.   I. Title.
   HN59.2.E29 2008
   973.93–dc22

                                                                    2008003384

Henry Holt books are available for special promotions and
premiums. For details contact: Director, Special Markets.
Originally published in hardcover in 2008 by Metropolitan Books
First Holt Paperbacks Edition 2009
Designed by Meryl Sussman Levavi
Printed in the United States of America
10   9   8   7   6   5   4   3   2   1

To all the under-celebrated people who
make books possible and available—
editorial assistants, copy editors,
proofreaders, publicists, print industry
workers, truck drivers, and
bookstore workers.

Contents

HELL DAY AT WORK

DECLINING HEALTH

GETTING SEX STRAIGHT

FALSE GODS

THIS
LAND
IS THEIR
LAND

Introduction

FOR A YEAR OR SO AT THE BEGINNING OF THE MILLEN-
nium, Americans were swept up in a spasm of unity.
We hadn't had an enemy scary enough to pull us together
since the USSR deconstructed in 1991, and now here was
one capable of bringing down the World Trade Center with
box cutters, a group that had declared they wanted every
one of us dead, from the janitors in our buildings to the
CEOs. Transfixed by the jihadists, we wrapped ourselves in
flags–flag sweaters, T-shirts, decals, lapel pins, even under-
wear and bathing suits. "United We Stand," proclaimed the
bumper stickers, and "These Colors Don't Run."

To be sure, this unity was as thin as a starlet after a
sojourn at a spa. How were we to express it, for example,
other than through our sartorial decisions? We pondered
the ubiquitous instruction to "report all suspicious persons

and activities" and that even more enigmatic command from the New York mass transit system: "See something, say something." The president advised us to carry on shopping, which we did to the best of our abilities, remaining in a state of dazed puzzlement while the TSA stripped off our shoes and our belts and the government ripped away habeas corpus and all the elementary ingredients of privacy.

But whatever resonated with us about the idea of a "homeland" and "one nation, indivisible" was being quietly undercut by a force more powerful than terrorism, more divisive than treason. In a process that had begun in the 1980s and suddenly accelerated in the 2000s, the ground was shifting under our feet, recarving the American landscape. The peaks of great wealth grew higher, rising up beyond the clouds, while the valleys of poverty sank lower into perpetual shadow. The once broad plateau of the middle class eroded away into a narrow ledge, with the white-knuckled occupants holding on for dear life.

It wasn't just a "shift," of course, governed by impersonal geological forces. The rude hand of human intervention could be felt in 2001, when the Bush government gave the airlines a $20 billion post-9/11 bail-out, with nothing for the ninety thousand freshly laid-off airline employees. In another deft upward redistribution of wealth, the administration cut taxes for the wealthiest Americans while cutting back on services and programs, such as financial aid, for everyone else. We had never had a gang in Washington as noisily committed to "Christian values," and yet they had managed to stand core biblical teachings on their head.

The results were glaringly visible by 2004, when the Democratic vice presidential candidate announced there were now "two Americas." This was almost certainly an undercount. We had divided into two markets—upscale and downscale, Saks and Sears—two decades earlier, and now these were further subdividing. The middle class, battered by wave after wave of outsourcings and layoffs, scrambled to meet the ever-rising costs of health care, fuel, and college education. The traditional working class, already savaged by deindustrialization, took the low-paying service jobs that were left, trading their hard hats for mops and trays. They crowded grown children and grandchildren into their homes, which they refinanced at usurious rates. They faced speedups at work and cutbacks in pay. When their monthly health insurance premiums exceeded the mortgage or rent, they abandoned the insurance and fell back on Advil.

As for the rich, mere millionaires and the old-money sorts who favor weather-beaten summer homes in Nantucket barely qualified anymore. The upper class split into the merely affluent, who shop at Williams-Sonoma, and the überrich, who had others do their shopping for them, as well as their child raising, bill paying, servant supervising, and party throwing. At the pinnacles of the wealth scale, extravagance reigned on a scale not seen since the late Roman Empire. Freshly fattened CEOs, hedge fund operators, and financiers hired interior decorators for their private jets, slugged back $10,000 martinis at the Algonquin Hotel in Manhattan, and, in one case, staged a $2 million birthday party in Sardinia featuring an ice statue of David urinating vodka.

There was a connection, as most people suspected, between the massive buildup of wealth among the few and the anxiety and desperation of the many. The money that fueled the explosion of gluttony at the top had to come from somewhere or, more specifically, from *someone.* Since no domestic oil deposits had been discovered, no new seams of uranium or gold, and since the war in Iraq enriched only the military contractors and suppliers, it had to have come from other Americans. In fact, the greatest capitalist innovations of the decade were in the realm of squeezing money out of those who had little to spare: taking away workers' pensions and benefits to swell profits, offering easy credit on dubious terms, raising insurance premiums and refusing to insure those who might ever make a claim, downsizing workforces to boost share prices, even falsifying time records to avoid paying overtime.

Prosperity, in America, had not always been a zero-sum game. Early twentieth-century capitalists—who were certainly no saints—envisioned a prosperous people generating profits for the upper class by buying houses and cars and washing machines. But somewhere along the line, the ethos changed from *we're all in this together* to *get what you can while the getting is good.* Let the environment decay, the infrastructure crumble, the public hospitals close, the schools get by on bake sales, the workers drop from exhaustion—who cares? Raise the premiums, reduce the wages, add new mystery fees to each bill, and let the devil take the hindmost. Only when the poor suckers at the bottom stopped buying and defaulted on their mortgages did anyone notice them.

And where were the rest of us during this orgy of accumulation at the top? What were we thinking as the invisible hand of the market reached into our pockets for our wallets? The truth is that most of us were too focused on the tasks at hand to pay much attention to what was going on with the neighbors. We were paying the bills, holding on to the job, occasionally making contact with the children. And when we did take a moment to tune into the public discourse, what we heard only worsened our frustration and pain.

The war with Iraq, for starters, which had to be one of the greatest non sequiturs in military history. Attacked by a gang composed largely of Islamic militants from Saudi Arabia, the United States countered by invading an unrelated country, and one of the most secular in the Middle East at that. Briefly fascinated by the toppling of statues and flattening of towns, we rallied to "support our troops," although no one could figure out what we were supporting them to do. If the war had been launched as a distraction from the corporate scandals of 2002, as one theory goes, it soon became something we needed distraction from. Five years into the war, and after the hideous revelations of Abu Ghraib, we'd spent $586 billion, lost more than four thousand American lives, and achieved the status of a pariah among nations.

Issues more appropriate to a middle school biology or sex ed class also loomed large. Stem cells, for example: whole political careers were based on the defense of these wee entities and their slightly larger cousins the embryos. Insentient forms of life, such as a woman in a vegetative state, excited loud indignation, while the intact and living received barely a nod. Gay marriage was another unlikely issue seemingly designed to distract us from the ongoing economic looting. How one person's marriage could threaten another's is a mystery to me, but whole elections were tipped in favor of the party of wealth, for no other purpose than to spare the public from the spectacle of same-sex embraces at the altar. As for the unmarried of any sexual orientation, abstinence was strongly recommended, along with prayer and cold showers.

Illegal immigrants were our perennial distraction, vilified as if they had come to run drugs and collect welfare rather than mow lawns, clean offices, pack meat, and process poultry. Welfare had gone, of course, and that may be what made the immigrants such an appealing target. Twenty years ago, right-wing demagogues had welfare recipients to kick around as a stand-in for the hated poor; in the aughts, immigrant workers were pressed into playing the scapegoat role. The strategy was the same: to peel off some segment of the poorer classes, label them as enemies, and try to whip up rage that might have been directed at the economic overclass. There may be reasonable arguments for limiting immigration, but it wasn't a Mexican who took away your pension or sold you on a dodgy mortgage.

Maybe, too, our critical faculties were dimmed by the habit, endemic in the 2000s, of magical thinking. One of the biggest self-help best sellers of the era tells you how you can have anything you want, simply by willing it, and the fiction side of the bookstore was ruled by a young magician in training. Girls forsook feminism for a princess fantasy that culminates in weddings lavish enough to bankrupt a couple before they can even take out a car loan. A White House aide derided the press for its membership in the "reality-based community," and the fastest-growing brand of religion was of the magical "name it and claim it" variety, in which the deity exists only to meet one's immediate, self-identified needs. How shortsighted it is to whine about rising debts and falling incomes when, with a little spiritual effort, the miraculous could happen to you.

How many "wake-up calls" do we need, people—how many broken levees, drowned cities, depleted food pantries, and people dead for lack of ordinary health care? As we approached the end of the first decade of the twenty-first century, we confronted a bleak landscape cluttered with boarded-up homes and littered with broken dreams. In the presidential election, the people dared to say it: The looting of America has gone on too long. The average American is too maxed out, overworked, and overspent to have anything left to take. The time has come for a new deal, a new distribution of power and wealth, if we want to restore the beautiful idea that was "America."

We have a choice. We can let the nation continue to fall apart, of course—dividing ever more clearly into the gated communities on the one hand and trailer parks and tenements on the other—until we eventually become one of those areas of the world prefixed by the mournful word *former.*

But I like to think we will find in our hearts some true ground for unity, some awareness of a common condition and collective aspiration. Maybe we will find it in an effort to restore America's lost glory—the beauty of our land before all the fences and sprawl, the respect we once enjoyed from people around the world. Or maybe we need to find it in the common threats we face, not only from the human enemies that our foreign policy has been breeding so prolifically but from the global challenge of climate change and shrinking supplies of water and oil. And maybe, someday, we will even regain the confidence to extend that sense of unity and connectedness to all of our fellow human beings, wherever they may reside on the planet.

CHASMS OF INEQUALITY

This Land Is Their Land

I RECENTLY TOOK A LITTLE BREAK—NINE HOURS IN SUN Valley before an evening speaking engagement. The sky was deep blue, the air crystalline, the hills green and, unlike much of the West, not yet on fire. Strolling out of the Sun Valley Lodge, I found a tiny tourist village, complete with Swiss-style bakery, multistar restaurant, and "opera house." What luck: the boutiques were displaying outdoor racks of summer clothing on sale! Nature and commerce were conspiring to make this the perfect microvacation.

But things started to get a little sinister—maybe I had wandered onto a movie set or Paris Hilton's closet?— because even at a 60 percent discount, I couldn't find a sleeveless cotton shirt for less than $100. These items shouldn't have been outdoors; they should have been in locked glass cases.

Then I remembered the general rule, still in place, even in a shaky economy: *if a place is truly beautiful, you can't afford to be there.* All right, I'm sure there are still exceptions, a few scenic spots not yet eaten up by mansions. But they're going fast.

About ten years ago, for example, a friend and I rented a snug, inexpensive one-bedroom house in Driggs, Idaho, just over the Tetons from wealthy Jackson Hole. At that time, Driggs was where the workers lived, driving over the Teton Pass every day to wait tables and make beds on the stylish side of the mountains. The point is, we low-rent folks got to wake up to the same scenery the rich people enjoyed and hike along the same pine-scented trails.

But the money was already starting to pour into Driggs— Paul Allen of Microsoft, August Busch III of Anheuser-Busch, Harrison Ford—transforming family potato farms into vast dynastic estates. I haven't been back, but I understand Driggs has become another unaffordable Jackson Hole. Where the waitstaff and bed makers live today I do not know.

I take this personally. I need to see vast expanses of water, 360-degree horizons, and mountains piercing the sky—at least for a week or two of the year. According to evolutionary psychologist Nancy Etcoff, we all do, and the need is hardwired into us. "People like to be on a hill, where they can see a landscape. And they like somewhere to go where they can *not* be seen themselves," she told *Harvard Magazine*. "That's a place desirable to a predator who wants to avoid becoming prey." We also like to be able to see water (for drinking), low-canopy trees (for shade), and animals (whose presence signals that the place is habitable).

But the gentrification of rural America has a downside for the wealthy too. The more expensive a resort town gets, the farther its workers have to commute to keep it functioning. And if your heart doesn't bleed for the dishwasher or landscaper who commutes two to four hours a day, at least shed a tear for the wealthy vacationer who gets stuck in the ensuing traffic. It's bumper to bumper westbound out of Telluride every day at five, or eastbound on Route 1 out of Key West, for the Lexuses as well as the beat-up old pickup trucks.

Then there's the elusive element of charm, which quickly drains away in a uniform population of multimillionaires. The Hamptons had their fishermen. Key West still advertises its "characters"—sun-bleached, weatherbeaten misfits who drifted down for the weather or to escape some difficult situation on the mainland. But the fishermen are long gone from the Hamptons and disappearing from Cape Cod. As for Key West's "characters," with the traditional little "conch houses" once favored by shrimpers going for a million and up, these human sources of local color have to be prepared to sleep with the scorpions under the highway overpass.

In Telluride, even a developer is complaining about the lack of affordable housing. "To have a real town," he told the *Financial Times*, "Telluride needs some locals hanging out"—in old-fashioned diners, for example, where you don't have to speak Italian to order a cup of coffee.

When I was a child, I sang "America the Beautiful" and meant it. I was born in the Rocky Mountains and raised, at various times, on the coasts. The Big Sky, the rolling surf, the jagged, snow-capped mountains—all this seemed to be my birthright. But now I flinch when I hear Woody Guthrie's line "This land belongs to you and me." Somehow, I don't think it was meant to be sung by a chorus of hedge fund operators.

Miami Vice: The Class Analysis

EVERYONE KNOWS THAT THE BIG-SCREEN *MIAMI VICE* was "darker" than the old television series, meaning that the lighthearted, wisecracking Don Johnson and Philip Michael Thomas were replaced by the brooding, inarticulate Colin Farrell and Jamie Foxx, who favor dingy blues and grays over their predecessors' lavender and turquoise outfits. But the real darkness of the movie went unnoted by the critics: in the movie *Vice*, Michael Mann offers up an economically globalized world populated only by the grimly poor and the breathtakingly ultrarich, all of whom are big-time felons.

Here, the poor serve largely as scenery, reminding us that we are now in Port au Prince (black faces), Ciudad del Este (brown), or a trailer park in the industrial wastelands of Miami (white and often tattooed). A few of them seem to be employed as lookouts or, a little higher up the career ladder, "shooters" for the drug gangs. Otherwise, they might as well be signposts.

As for a middle or working class, in crime fiction this is the historical role of the cops or private eyes. In *Miami Vice*, though, the good guys have not a shred of material existence to betray their social class. Crockett and Tubbs don't live anywhere and touch down only in unfurnished apartments provided by their employer, where they use the showers for sex. They never sleep or eat, so we cannot know whether they prefer, for example, burgers to blackened sea bass. Only bad guys eat, and then not much. The one who did appear to be chewing may have been just gnawing on his meth mouth.

In general, it's a starkly stripped-down world our heroes now inhabit. What is all the shooting about? Drugs, of course, but these are rarely mentioned by name, nor do the good guys ever hint at any moral impulse for the war. Are the drugs destructive? Could they possibly be more destructive than the shoot-outs, bombings, and torturings occasioned by their illegal status? No one seems to care. Drugs are just the "product," and the only issue is their delivery—successful or intercepted in a hail of automatic weapon fire.

In Mann's hyperabstract version of global capitalism, the product could be anything, so long as its price is high enough. To make sure we get the point, the coldhearted drug queen played by Gong Li suits up in high-corporate minimalism and refers to herself as a "businesswoman."

It's the ultrarich—Gong Li and her colleagues—who hold our eyes in *Miami Vice*. They live too large for movies; they need IMAX. I gasped when the camera swept over Brazil's Iguassu Falls, which are surely the very suburbs of heaven, and settled on the evil ones' mountain-top mansion, where the drug lord and his lady were cuddling and scheming, attended by a small army of servants. They may not have much fun—Gong Li's thoughts are elsewhere—but whatever else they have, they have it fast. Want to dash over to Geneva to make a deposit? The personal jet awaits.

There's an instructive scene when things begin to heat up between Colin Farrell and Gong Li. (They're on opposite sides of the drug war but in the same zone of hotness.) He offers her a drink. She favors mojitos and tells him the best ones are in Havana. They're in Miami when this exchange takes place, but no problem, a high-speed power boat whisks them off to the mojito source. If she'd asked for a Stoli on million-year-old ice, no doubt they would have hightailed it right down to Antarctica.

All right, it's just a silly movie, lacking either comprehensible dialogue or plot. But Mann's bleak vision of a world divided between shanty towns and trailer parks at one end and unimaginable luxury at the other is not far off the mark. Take the crucial matter of travel: while the poor creep around in buses and the affluent creep a little faster in taxis, there's a class of people who take helicopters to the airport, where they then embark on private planes. According to the *New York Times*, private aviation has gone "mainstream," with even the "merely rich," who can't afford their own planes, buying up twenty-five hours of air travel for $299,000.

No pretzels on their menu. As the *Times* reports, one private fleet met a passenger's requirement for "Grey Goose vodka frozen two hours before flight; ice cubes made with Fiji water; filet mignon of precise cut and dimension; and Froot Loops . . . for the kids."

Meanwhile, according to globalissues.com, nearly half the world's people—three billion—live on less than $2 a day. Their lives are too cramped and squalid to make for good summer viewing. But they do serve a cinematic function by catching the occasional bullet or bomb.

Home Depot's CEO-Size Tip

I'M NOT UPSET BY ALL THOSE MULTI-MILLION-DOLLAR GOLDEN parachutes CEOs have been picking up lately. Not at all. Take the $210 million Robert Nardelli received as a send-off from Home Depot. To those critics who see it as one more step in the slide from free-market capitalism to a gluttonous free-for-all, I say: What do you really know about Nardelli's circumstances? Maybe he has a dozen high-maintenance ex–trophy wives to support, each with a brood of special-needs offspring. Ever think of what that would cost?

Or he may have a rare disease that can be held at bay only by daily infusions of minced fresh gorilla liver. Just try purchasing a gorilla a day for purposes of personal consumption—or any other endangered species, for that matter. There are the poachers to pay, the smugglers, the doctors and vets. I'm just saying: Don't start envisioning offshore bank accounts and 50,000-square-foot fourth homes until you know the whole story.

Another reason I'm not troubled by the $210 million payoff is that the Home Depot board may think of it as a kind of tip for its fired CEO, and like me, they may not feel tips need to be linked to performance. I don't tip as a reward for good service; I give a tip because it's part of the tipped person's living. Waitstaff, for example, earn about $2 or $3 an hour—a bit more now in certain states—so a tip is just my contribution to their wage. Sloppy waitress? Surly cabdriver? I'm not their supervisor—they get their 20–25 percent anyway.

So what if Home Depot's stock fell from $50 to $41 on Nardelli's watch? Maybe the board should be commended for their generous tipping policies. Possibly they're trying to send a message to us stingy 20 percenters: that 300 percent (based on Nardelli's $64 million earnings over his six-year tenure) is more like it.

Or it could be that Home Depot has a more profound philosophical message to impart. The board may have decided to flout the very principle of capitalist exchange: that what you get paid should in some way reflect the work that you've done—or the "value added," as they say in the business. Other companies are taking the same antimarket approach. Pfizer rewarded its failed CEO with an exit package of $200 million, and Merrill Lynch's Stan O'Neal got a $161.5 million retirement package after presiding over that company's $8.4 million write-down of mortgage-related losses.

Picture the board members sitting cross-legged on the floor in a circle, munching s'mores and giggling about how cleverly they've undermined the basis of our capitalist economy. Home Depot sales clerks get about $8–10 an hour for lifting heavy objects and running around the floor all day; the CEO gets a total of almost $300 million for sinking the stock. We're not talking about a rational system of rewards—just random acts of kindness, vast sums of money alighting when and where they will, generally in the outstretched hands of those who already have far too much.

Going to Extremes:
CEOs vs. Slaves

RECENT FINDINGS SHED NEW LIGHT ON THE INCREAS-ingly unequal terrain of American society. Starting at the top executive level, you may have thought, as I did, that the guys in the C suites operated as a team—or, depending on your point of view, a pack or gang—each getting his fair share of the take. But no, the rising tide in executive pay does not lift all yachts equally. The latest pay gap to worry about is the one between the CEO and his—or very rarely her—third in command.

According to a study by Carola Frydman of the Massachusetts Institute of Technology and Raven E. Saks at the Federal Reserve, thirty to forty years ago the CEOs of major companies earned 80 percent more, on average, than the third-highest-paid executives. By the early part of the twenty-first century, however, the gap between the CEO and the third in command had ballooned up to 260 percent.

Now take a look at what's happening at the very bottom of the economic spectrum, where you might have pictured low-wage workers trudging between food banks or mendicants dwelling in cardboard boxes. It turns out, though, that the bottom is a lot lower than that. In May 2007, a millionaire couple in a woodsy Long Island suburb was charged with keeping two Indonesian domestics as slaves for five years, during which the women were paid $100 a month, fed very little, forced to sleep on mats on the floor, and subjected to beatings, cigarette burns, and other torments.

This is hardly an isolated case. If the new "top" involves pay in the tens or hundreds of millions, a private jet, and a few acres of Marin County, the new bottom is slavery. Some of America's slaves are captive domestics like the Indonesian women on Long Island. Others are sweatshop or restaurant workers, and at least ten thousand are sex slaves lured from their home countries to American brothels by the promise of respectable jobs.

CEOs and slaves: these are the extreme ends of American class polarization. But a parallel splitting is going on in many of the professions. Top-ranked college professors, for example, enjoy salaries of several hundred thousand a year, often augmented by consulting fees and earnings from their patents or biotech companies. At the other end of the professoriate, you have adjunct teachers toiling away for about $5,000 a semester or less, with no benefits or chance of tenure. There was a story a few years ago about an adjunct who commuted to his classes from a homeless shelter in Manhattan, and adjuncts who moonlight as waitresses or cleaning ladies are legion.

Similarly, the legal profession, which is topped by law firm partners billing hundreds of dollars an hour, now has a new proletariat of temp lawyers working for $19–25 an hour in sweatshop conditions. On sites like http://temporaryattorney .blogspot.com/, temp lawyers report working twelve hours a day, six days a week, in crowded basements with inadequate sanitary facilities. According to an article in *American Lawyer*, a legal temp at a major New York firm reported being "corralled in a windowless basement room littered with dead cockroaches" where six out of seven exits were blocked.

Contemplating the violent and increasing polarization of American society, one cannot help but think of "dark energy," the mysterious force that is propelling the galaxies apart from one another at a speed far greater than can be accounted for by the energy of the original big bang. Cosmic bodies seem to be repelling one another, much as a CEO must look down at his CFO and COO, etc., and think, "They're getting too close. I've got to make more, more, more!"

The difference is that the galaxies don't need one another and are free to go their separate ways nonchalantly. But the CEO presumably depends on his fellow executives, just as the star professor relies on adjuncts to do his or her teaching and the law firm partner is enriched by the sweated labor of legal temps. For all we know, some of those CEOs go home to sip their single malts in mahogany-walled dens that have been cleaned by domestic slaves.

Why is it so hard for the people at the top to graciously acknowledge their dependency on the labor of others? We need some sort of gravitational force to counter the explosive distancing brought about by greed—before our economy imitates the universe and blows itself to smithereens.

Banish the Bloated Overclass

TWENTY YEARS AGO IT WAS RISKY TO POINT OUT THE growing inequality in America. I did it in a *New York Times* essay and was quickly denounced, in the *Washington Times*, as a "Marxist." If only. I've never been able to get through more than a couple of pages of *Das Kapital*, even in English, and the *Grundrisse* functions like Rozerem.

But it no longer takes a Marxist, real or alleged, to see that America is being polarized between the superrich few and the subrich everyone else. According to the *New York Times Magazine*, even Larry Summers, the centrist Democratic economist and former Harvard president, is now obsessed with the statistic that, since 1979, the share of pretax income going to the top 1 percent of American households has risen by 7 percentage points, to 16 percent. At the same time, the share of income going to the bottom 80 percent has fallen by 7 percentage points.

As the *Times* puts it: "It's as if every household in that bottom 80 percent is writing a check for $7,000 every year and sending it to the top 1 percent." Summers now admits that his former cheerleading for the corporate-dominated global economy feels like "pretty thin gruel."

But the moderate-to-conservative economists who refuse to think about class polarization have a fallback position, sketched out by financial journalist Roger Lowenstein in an essay in the same issue of the *New York Times*. Briefly put, as long as the middle class is still trudging along and the poor are not starving flamboyantly in the streets, what does it matter if the superrich are absorbing an ever-larger share of the national income?

In Lowenstein's view, "whether Roger Clemens, who will get something like $10,000 for every pitch he throws, earns 100 times or 200 times what I earn is kind of irrelevant. My kids still have health care, and they go to decent schools. It's not the rich people who are pulling away at the top who are the problem."

Well, yes, they *are*, and in several ways. A bloated overclass can drag down a society as surely as a swelling underclass.

First, the Clemens example distracts from the reality that a great deal of the wealth at the top is built on the low-wage labor of the poor. Take Wal-Mart, our largest private employer and premiere exploiter of the working class. Every year, four or five of the people on *Forbes* magazine's list of the twenty richest Americans carry the surname Walton, meaning they are the children, nieces, and nephews of Wal-Mart's founder. You think it's a coincidence that this union-busting low-wage retail empire happens to have generated a $65 billion family fortune?

Second, though a lot of today's wealth is being made in the financial industry, by means that are occult to the average citizen and do not seem to involve much labor of any kind, we all pay a price somewhere down the line. All those late fees, puffed-up interest rates, and exorbitant charges for low-balance checking accounts do not, as far as I can determine, go to soup kitchens.

Third, the overclass bids up the price of goods that ordinary people also need—housing, for example. Gentrification is dispersing the urban poor into overcrowded suburban ranch houses, while billionaires' horse farms displace the rural poor and middle class. Similarly, the rich can swallow tuitions of $40,000 and up, making a college education increasingly a privilege of the upper classes.

Finally, and perhaps most important, the huge concentration of wealth at the top is routinely used to tilt the political process in favor of the wealthy. Yes, we should acknowledge the philanthropic efforts of exceptional billionaires like George Soros and Bill Gates. But if we don't end up with universal health insurance in the next few years, it won't be because the average American isn't pining for relief from escalating medical costs. It may well turn out to be because Hillary Clinton is, as the *Nation* reports, "the number-one Congressional recipient of donations from the healthcare industry." And who do you think demanded those Bush tax cuts for the wealthy—the AFL-CIO?

Lowenstein does note that "if the very upper crust were banished to a Caribbean island, the America that remained would be a lot more egalitarian." Well, duh. The point is that it would also be more prosperous, at the individual level, and more democratic. In fact, why give the upper crust an island in the Caribbean? After all they've done for us recently, I think the Aleutians should be more than adequate.

Got Grease?

I T'S NOT ONLY THE STOCK MARKET THAT HAS THE UPPER classes biting their fingernails. In the last few years, the low-fat, high-carb way of life that was central to the self-esteem of the affluent has been all but discredited. If avarice was the principal vice of the bourgeoisie, a commitment to low fat was its counterbalancing virtue. You can bet, for example, that those CEOs who cooked the books and ransacked their companies' assets did not start the day with two eggs over easy, a rasher of bacon, and a side of hash browns. No, unbuttered low-fat muffins and delicate slices of melon fueled the crimes of Wall Street: grease was for proles.

But that dogma no longer holds up. A large number of nutritionists now deny that the low-fat approach will make you slim and resistant to heart disease. As we know, the onset of the American epidemic of obesity coincided precisely with the arrival of the antifat campaign in the 1980s, accompanied by a cornucopia of low-fat cookies, cakes, potato chips, and frozen pot roast dinners. Millions of Americans began to pig out on "guilt-free" feasts of ungarnished carbs—with perverse and often debilitating results, especially among those unable to afford health club memberships and long hours on the elliptical trainer.

I have confirmed these findings with my own scientific study, which draws on a sample of exactly two: Jane Brody, the *New York Times* health columnist and tireless opponent of all foodstuffs other than veggies and starch, and me. It was Brody, more than anyone else, who promoted the low-fat way of life to the masses, from the eighties on, with headlines like "Our Excessive Protein Intake Can Hurt Liver, Kidneys, Bone," "Fill Up on Bread to Lose Weight," and "Chemicals in Food Less Harmful Than Fat."

As she revealed in a 1999 column, Brody was herself raised on a high-carb, low-fat diet of "shredded wheat, oatmeal, challah, Jewish rye and bagels," the last, presumably, unblemished by the customary "shmear" of cream cheese. I, meanwhile, was raised on a diet that might strain even an Inuit's gall bladder. We ate eggs every morning, meat for lunch, and meat again for dinner, invariably accompanied by gravy or at least pan drippings. We buttered everything from broccoli to brownies and would have buttered butter itself if it were not for the problems of traction presented by the butter-butter interface.

And how did Brody and I exit from our dietarily opposite childhoods? She, by her own admission, was a veritable butterball by her midtwenties—a size 14 at just under five feet tall. I, at five foot seven, weighed in at a gaunt and geeky 110 pounds.

Fast-forwarding to the present, we assume Brody is now admirably trim, if only because of her exercise regimen, since otherwise she wouldn't have dared to promote the low-fat dogma in person. For my part, I no longer butter my brownies, perhaps in part because of Brody's tireless preaching. But the amount of fat she recommends for an entire day—one tablespoon—wouldn't dress a small salad for me or lubricate a single Triscuit. I still regard bread as a vehicle for butter and chicken as an excuse for gravy or, when served cold, mayonnaise. The result? I'm a size 6 and have a cholesterol level that an envious doctor once denounced as "too low." Case closed.

But if that doesn't convince you, there's now a solid medical explanation for why the low-fat, high-carb approach is actually fattening. A meal of carbs—especially those derived from sugar and refined flour—is followed by a surge of blood sugar, then, as insulin is released in response, a sudden collapse, leaving you often lightheaded, cranky, headachy, and certainly hungrier than before you ate. Fats and protein can make you fat too, of course, if ingested in sufficient quantity, but at least they fulfill the conventional role of anything designated as a foodstuff, which is to say that they leave you feeling like you've actually eaten something.

As long as people want to lose weight, we'll probably have dueling diet doctors. But now that it's apparent that the prevailing low-fat wisdom is bunk, why would anyone opt for a diet with a mouthfeel that mimics sawdust?

Perhaps because facts don't matter when a dogma so flattering to the affluent is at stake. In the last couple of decades, the low-fat way of life has become an important indicator of social rank, along with whole-grain—as opposed to white—bread and natural fibers versus polyester. If you doubt this, consider the multiple meanings of *grease*, as in *greaser* and *greasy spoon.* Among the nutritionally correct upper-middle-class people of my acquaintance, a dinner of French bread and pasta has long been considered a suitable offering for guests—followed by a plate of bone-dry biscotti. And don't bother asking for the butter.

What has made the low-fat dogma especially impervious to critique, though, is the overclass identification of low-fat with virtue and fat with the long-suspected underclass tendency to self-indulgence. Low-fat is the flip side of avarice for a reason: thanks to America's deep streak of Puritanism—perhaps mixed with a dollop of democratic idealism—ours has been a culture in which everyone wants to be rich but no one wants to be known as a "fat cat." We might be hogging the earth's resources, the affluent seem to be saying, but at least we're not indulging the ancient human craving for fat. So the low-fat diet has been the hair shirt under the fur coat—the daily deprivation that offsets the endless greed.

I wouldn't go so far as to blame the financial shenanigans of the last few years on Brody, but clearly there is a connection. The long-term effects of a low-fat, low-protein diet are easy to guess—a perpetual feeling of insatiety, a relentless, gnawing hunger for more. No doubt, for many thousands of low-fat, high-earning people, money became a substitute, however unfulfilling, for dietary fat. The effect was naturally strongest in Silicon Valley, where dot-com mania collided with the Northern California, Berkeley-based carbo cult, to disastrous effect. That "irrational exuberance" of the late nineties was in fact the giddiness of hypoglycemia, induced by a diet of boutique muffins and $5-a-loaf "artisan bread."

My advice to the fat-deprived execs: Take a break from

the markets and go out and get yourself a bacon cheeseburger and fries or, if you still have a few bucks to toss
around, a nice pancetta-rich plate of spaghetti carbonara.
Eat every last drop. Then lean back, with the grease drip-
ping down your chin, smile at the people around you, and
appreciate, perhaps for the very first time, what it feels like
to have enough.

Class Struggle 101

WELCOME TO HIGHER EDUCATION, TWENTY-FIRST-century style, where the most important course offered is not listed in the college catalog. It's called Class Struggle, and it pits the men in suits—administrators and trustees—against the men and women who keep the school running: maintenance workers, groundskeepers, clerical and technical workers, housekeepers, food service workers. In the last few years, there've been student activities in support of workers at dozens of campuses, including Yale, Stanford, Georgetown, Temple, the University of Virginia, the University of Pennsylvania, and New York University. At Miami University of Ohio, when 460 maintenance workers went out on strike, the students erected a tent city in front of the administration building, and faculty members spent a night there in solidarity. As part of the campaign, union picketers humiliated the university by turning away the union camera crews who had come to televise the Miami RedHawks–Cincinnati Bearcats game.

College presidents, deans, provosts, chancellors–along with their deputies, assistants, and other members of the ever-proliferating educational administrative workforce–insist that their labor problems are a sorry distraction from their institutions' noble purpose of enlightening young minds. But administrators like to cloak themselves in the moral authority of Western civilization, such as it is, which means that labor issues are hardly peripheral to the university's educational mission. On an increasing number of campuses, for example, incoming students are greeted at a formal fall convocation in which the top administrators–suited up in full medieval mortarboard-and-gown attire–deliver platitudinous speeches about Character, Integrity, and Truth. The message is that these weirdly costumed folks are not mere executives of a corporation but the guardians of an ancient and sacred tradition. So when these same dignitaries turn out to be grossly underpaying their employees and harassing the "troublemakers" among them, they do so with the apparent blessing of Aristotle, Plato, and Shakespeare.

If the university has so much to teach about social inequality, why shouldn't the students get credit for learning it? The covert lessons from the administration should be formalized as course offerings, such as:

- Elementary Class Structure of the United States: The University as Microcosm. In this 4-credit course, we will examine the pay gradient from housekeeper (approximately $19,000/year) to president (ranging up to $1,411,894 for Columbia's Lee Bollinger). In the final exam, students will be asked to discuss the rationale for this pay gap in terms of the payees' contributions to the university, ongoing housing and wardrobe expenses, and intrinsic human worth.

- Presidential Architecture: A 3-credit seminar course featuring field trips through university-provided presidential dwellings, including "great rooms," wet bars, saunas, guest suites, and exercise rooms, with a side trip, if time permits, to the trailer parks favored by the housekeeping and maintenance staff.

- Race, Gender, and Occupational Preference: In this advanced sociology seminar, we will analyze the way campus workers sort themselves into various occupations on the basis of race and gender and will explore various theories attempting to explain this phenomenon—for example, the Innate Athleticism theory of why African Americans so often prefer manual labor and the Nimble Fingers theory of why females can usually be found doing the clerical work.

- Topics in University Financing: A 4-credit business course tracing the development of the current two-pronged approach to financing institutions of higher learning: tuition increases for the students plus pay decreases for the staff. Alternative approaches to financing, featuring militant campaigns for adequate public funding for higher education, will be thoroughly critiqued.

A cynic might say that the true purpose of college is to teach exactly such lessons. After all, college graduates are a relative elite, constituting only 25 percent of the adult population and expected to fill the sorts of administrative and managerial jobs in which it is a positive advantage to be able to starve workers, impose layoffs, and bust unions without losing a minute of sleep. Some students catch on with lightninglike speed, such as Yale's precocious Scott Wexler, eighteen, who confided to the *New York Times*, "I kind of like walking through the picket lines." This young man will make a fine assistant regional manager at Target—or possibly a college president.

Fortunately, not all students are buying the administrations' lesson plan. At Harvard, students occupied an administration building for twenty-one days to persuade the administration to bargain with campus janitors, many of whom were paid only $6.50 an hour. Stanford students went on a hunger strike in support of campus blue-collar workers. And it's not just the superelite schools that have generated vigorous student-labor alliances. At mainstream public universities like those of Maryland and Virginia, there are plenty of students who would agree with Miami University's Justin Katko when he writes that he got involved in the campus workers' struggle because "I could not allow such extreme disparities as are found on college campuses . . . to exist without being ashamed of myself for apathy."

It's hard to concentrate in classrooms that are cleaned during the night by people who can barely make rent. And when the cafeteria staff have to work second jobs to feed their own children, you tend to choke on your chicken fingers.

Minimum Wage Rises,
Sky Does Not Fall

W HEN I RECENTLY FLEW TO SEATTLE, AIRPORT SECU-
rity gave me trouble over the four-pound ham I was
carrying. Several TSA officials gathered to consider the
question of whether ham is a "gel," to which I retorted: If
ham is a gel, so am I. I suggested that they biopsy it for
hidden box cutters. I offered to divide it into twenty-one
three-ounce chunks, each appropriately stowed in a Ziploc
baggie. But no deal.

So I broke down and told them I was flying into what I
had been warned would be a food-scarce zone: Washington
State, with a minimum wage of $7.93 an hour, could hardly
be expected to have affordable restaurants or a functioning
economy of any kind. Notable conservative economists
have almost unanimously predicted that an increased minimum wage will result in wild price increases and mass
unemployment, and I had a suitcase full of clippings to
prove it.

I would be entering a culinary wasteland, facing fast

food meals of $20 and up, and if I tried to fall back on soup kitchens, thousands of unemployed restaurant workers would be lined up ahead of me. Bringing my own ham seemed prudent, at the very least.

So imagine my surprise when I arrived, hamless, in Seattle to find it fully functional, if not positively bustling. Restaurants were packed, and I could still get a grilled salmon sandwich for $7.95 at a cafeteria-style place overlooking the sound. My hotel was amply staffed with congenial people and—perhaps only because of the un-Seattle-like cold, no beggars approached me on the streets. Nor can you argue that the dire effects of a higher minimum wage just haven't had time to set in: Washington raised its minimum wage above the federal level of $5.15 an hour about a decade ago.

In fact, according to the *New York Times*, Washington's economy was booming, generating ninety thousand new jobs in 2006 alone. Even business groups have stopped griping about the state's minimum wage. The article quotes a pizza store owner in the western part of the state: "We're paying the highest wage we've ever had to pay, and our business is still up more than 11 percent over last year."

My next stop was in California, with a minimum wage of $7.50 an hour, slated to go up to $8 in 2008. Again, no imported ham was required. Sidewalk taquerias flourished, as well as, or so I'm told, those celebrity sushi spots where you can pay $100 for a bite of fresh chum.

Overall, twenty-nine states have raised their minimum wages above $5.15 an hour, and—lo!—the sky has not fallen. Could we have some apologies, please, from the economists who predicted a retail apocalypse?

Not that a $7 or even $8 minimum wage is utopian. In the Seattle area, a "living wage" (calculated to reflect local housing and other basic costs) is $11.89 an hour for a single person and $25.35 for a family of three—more than three times the current minimum wage. Nationwide, it would take a wage of $16.31 an hour to afford a two-bedroom apartment.

There is no moral justification for a minimum wage lower than a living wage. And given the experience of the twenty-nine states that have raised their minimum wages, there isn't even an amoral economic justification either.

Could You Afford to Be Poor?

THERE ARE PEOPLE, CONCENTRATED IN MANHATTAN'S Upper East Side and Beverly Hills, who still confuse poverty with the simple life. No cable TV, no altercations with the maid, no summer home maintenance issues—just the basics, like family, sunsets, and walks in the park. What they don't know is that it's expensive to be poor. In fact, you, the reader of middling income, could probably not afford it.

A 2006 study from the Brookings Institution documents the "ghetto tax," or higher cost of living in low-income urban neighborhoods. It comes at you from every direction, from food prices to auto insurance. A few examples from this study, by Matt Fellowes, that covered twelve American cities:

- Poor people are less likely to have bank accounts, which can be expensive for those with low balances, and so they tend to cash their pay checks at check-cashing businesses, which, in the cities surveyed, charged $5 to $50 for a $500 check.

- Nationwide, low-income car buyers, defined as people earning less than $30,000 a year, pay 2 percentage points more for a car loan than more affluent buyers.
- Low-income drivers pay more for car insurance. In New York, Baltimore, and Hartford, they pay an average $400 more a year to insure the exact same car and driver risk as wealthier drivers.
- Poorer people pay an average of 1 percentage point more in mortgage interest.
- They are more likely to buy their furniture and appliances through pricey rent-to-own businesses. In Wisconsin, the study reports, a $200 rent-to-own TV set can cost $700 with the interest included.
- They are less likely to have access to large supermarkets and hence to rely on the far more expensive, and lower quality offerings, of small grocery and convenience stores.

I didn't live in any ghettoes when I worked on *Nickel and Dimed*—a trailer park, yes, but no ghetto—and on my average wage of $7 an hour, or about $14,400 a year, I wasn't in the market for furniture, a house, or a car. But the high cost of poverty was brought home to me within a few days of my entry into the low-wage life, when, slipping into social worker mode, I chastised a coworker for living in a motel room when it would be so much cheaper to rent an apartment. Her response: Where would she get the first month's rent and security deposit it takes to pin down an apartment? The lack of that amount of capital—probably well over $1,000— condemned her to paying $40 a night at the Day's Inn.

Then there was the problem of sustenance. I had gone into the project imagining myself preparing vast quantities of cheap, nutritious soups and stews, which I would freeze and heat for dinner each day. But surprise: I didn't have the proverbial pot to pee in, not to mention spices or Tupperware. A scouting trip to Kmart established that it would take about a $40 capital investment to get my kitchenette up to speed for the low-wage way of life.

The food situation got only more challenging when I, too, found myself living in a motel. Lacking a fridge and microwave, I had to get all my food from the nearest convenience store (hardboiled eggs and banana for breakfast) or, for the big meal of the day, Wendy's or KFC. I have no nutritional complaints; after all, there is a veggie, or flecks of one, in Wendy's broccoli and cheese baked potato. The problem was financial. A double cheeseburger and fries is a lot more expensive than that hypothetical homemade lentil stew.

There are other tolls along the road well traveled by the working poor. If your credit is lousy, which it is likely to be, you'll pay a higher deposit for a phone. If you don't have health insurance, you may end up taking that feverish child to an emergency room, and please don't think of ERs as socialized medicine for the poor. The average cost of a visit is over $1,000, which is more than ten times what a clinic pediatrician would charge. Or you neglect that hypertension, diabetes, or mystery lump until you end up with a $100,000 problem on your hands.

So let's have a little less talk about how the poor should learn to manage their money, and a little more attention to all the ways that money is being systematically siphoned off. Yes, certain kinds of advice would be helpful: skip the payday loans and rent-to-pay furniture, for example. But we need laws in more states to stop predatory practices like $50 charges for check cashing. Also, think what some microcredit could do to move families from motels and shelters to apartments. And did I mention a living wage?

If you're rich, you might want to stay that way. It's a whole lot cheaper than being poor.

Desperately Seeking Stimulus

WITH ALL THE TALK ABOUT HOW TO STIMULATE IT, you'd think that the economy is a giant sex organ. Ben Bernanke may not employ this imagery, but the immediate challenge—and the issue that replaced Iraq and immigration in the presidential race—is how best to get the economy engorged and throbbing again.

It would be irresponsible to say much about the last administration's stimulus plan, the mere mention of which was enough to send the Nikkei, the DAX, and the curiously named Sensex and FTSE tumbling into the crash zone. In a typically regressive gesture, Bush proposed to hand out cash tax rebates—except to families earning less than $40,000 a year. This may qualify as an example of what Naomi Klein calls "disaster capitalism," in which any misfortune can be rejiggered to the advantage of the affluent.

But even the liberal stimulus proposals have me worried—not so much for their content as for their rationale. Most liberals want a stimulus package that includes an increase in food stamp allotments and an extension of unemployment benefits, which are both screamingly obvious measures. Currently, the food stamp allotment amounts to about $1 per meal, and when four Democratic congresspersons tried living on that for a week they ended up even crankier than if they'd had to sit through a week-long filibuster by Tom DeLay.

As for unemployment benefits: they last just twenty-five weeks in most states and end up covering only a third of people who are laid off. If ever there was a time to create a real working system of unemployment compensation, it is now.

The economic rationale for a more progressive stimulus package is that the poor and the freshly unemployed will spend whatever money they get. Give them more money in the form of food stamps or unemployment benefits and they'll drop more at the mall. Money, it has been observed, sticks to the rich but just slides off the poor, which makes them the linchpin of stimulus. After decades of being stereotyped as lazy, stupid, addicted, and crime-prone, the poor have been discovered to have this singular virtue: they are veritable spending machines.

All this is true, but it is also a form of economy fetishism—or should I say worship? If we have learned anything in the last few years, it is that the economy is no longer an effective measure of human well-being. We've seen the economy grow without wage gains; we've seen productivity grow without wage gains. We've even seen unemployment fall without wage gains. In fact, when economists want to talk about life "on the ground," where jobs and wages and the price of Special K are paramount, they've taken to talking about "the real economy." If there's a "real economy," then what in the hell is "the economy"?

Once it was realer, this economy that we have. But that was before we got polarized into the rich, the poor, and the sinking middle class. Gross social inequality is what has "decoupled" growth and productivity from wage gains for the average household. As far as I can tell, "the economy," as opposed to "the real economy," is the realm of investment, and is occupied by people who live on interest and dividends instead of salaries and wages, aka the rich.

So I'm proposing a radical shift in rhetoric: any stimulus package should focus on the poor and the unemployed, not because they spend more but because they are most in need of help. Yes, when a parent can afford to buy Enfamil, it helps the Enfamil company and no doubt "the economy," too. But let's not throw out the baby with the sensual bubble bath of "stimulus." In any ordinary moral calculus, the baby comes first.

Far be it from me to make the revolutionary suggestion that babies are more important than profits. My point is just that our economy—with its dizzying bubbles, wild lending sprees, reckless downsizings, and planetwide hypersensitivity—has gotten too far disconnected from ordinary human needs. We could take our ongoing crisis as an opportunity to fix that, at least in part, by shoring up government support for the needy and the dislocated. Or we can wait around and watch while the imagery gets nasty, as this ghostly creature "the economy" starts acting like a sex addict in withdrawal.

Smashing Capitalism

SOMEWHERE IN THE HAMPTONS A HIGH ROLLER IS cursing his cleaning lady and shaking his fist at the lawn guys. The American poor, who are usually tactful enough to remain invisible to the multimillionaire class, suddenly leaped onto the scene and started smashing the global financial system. Incredibly enough, this may be the first case in history in which the downtrodden manage to bring down an unfair economic system without going to the trouble of a revolution.

First they stopped paying their mortgages, a move in which they were joined by many financially stretched middle-class folks, though the poor definitely led the way. All right, these were trick mortgages, many of them designed to be unaffordable within two years of signing the contract. There were "Ninja" loans, for example, awarded to people with "no income, no job or assets." Conservative pundits have been lamenting the low levels of "economic literacy" that allowed people to be exploited by subprime loans. Why didn't these low-income folks get lawyers to go over the fine print? And don't they have personal financial advisers anyway?

Then, in a diabolically clever move, the poor—a category which now roughly coincides with the working class—stopped shopping. Both Wal-Mart and Home Depot announced disappointing second-quarter performances in 2007, plunging the market into another Arctic-style meltdown. H. Lee Scott, CEO of the low-wage Wal-Mart empire, admitted with admirable sensitivity that "it's no secret that many customers are running out of money at the end of the month."

I wish I could report that the current attack on capitalism represents a deliberate strategy on the part of the poor, that there have been secret meetings in break rooms and parking lots around the country, where cell leaders issued instructions like, "You, Vinny—don't make any mortgage payment this month. And Caroline, forget that back-to-school shopping, OK?" But all the evidence suggests that the current crisis is something the high rollers brought down on themselves.

When, for example, the largest private employer in America, which is Wal-Mart, starts experiencing a shortage of customers, it needs to take a long, hard look in the mirror. About a century ago, Henry Ford realized that his company would prosper only if his own workers earned enough to buy Fords. Wal-Mart, on the other hand, never seemed to figure out that its cruelly low wages would eventually curtail its own growth, even at the company's famously discounted prices.

The sad truth is that people earning Wal-Mart-level wages tend to favor the fashions available at the Salvation

Army. Nor do they have much use for Wal-Mart's other departments, such as electronics, lawn and garden, and pharmacy.

It gets worse, though. While with one hand the high rollers, H. Lee Scott among them, squeezed the American worker's wages, the other hand was reaching out with the tempting offer of credit. In fact, easy credit became the American substitute for decent wages. Once you worked for your money, but now you were supposed to *pay* for it. Once you could count on earning enough to save for a home. Now you'll never earn that much, but, as the lenders were saying–heh, heh–do we have a mortgage for you!

Payday loans, rent-to-buy furniture, and exorbitant credit card interest rates for the poor were just the beginning. In a May 2007 cover story on "The Poverty Business," *Business Week* documented the stampede, in just the last few years, to lend money to the people who could least afford to pay the interest: Buy your dream home! Refinance your house! Take on a car loan even if your credit rating sucks! *Financiamos a todos!* Somehow, no one bothered to figure out where the poor were going to get the money to pay for all the money they were being offered.

Personally, I prefer my revolutions to be a little more proactive. There should be marches and rallies, banners and sit-ins, possibly a nice color theme like red or orange. Certainly, there should be a vision of what you intend to replace the bad old system with–European-style social democracy, Latin American–style socialism, or how about just American capitalism with some regulation thrown in?

Global capitalism will survive the current credit crisis; already the government has rushed in to soothe the feverish markets. But in the long term, a system that depends on extracting every last cent from the poor cannot hope for a healthy prognosis. Who would have thought that foreclosures in Stockton and Cleveland would roil the markets of London and Shanghai? The poor have risen up and spoken—only it sounds less like a shout of protest than a low, strangled cry for help.

The Communist
Manifesto Hits 160

2008 MARKED THE 160TH ANNIVERSARY OF THE *COMMU-nist Manifesto*, and capitalism, aka "free enterprise," seems willing to observe the occasion by dropping dead. Some pundits have started warning that the ATMs might run dry and hinting that the only safe investment left is canned beans. Apocalypse, or another attempt to extort bailout money for the banks? No one seems to know, though the populist part of the populace has been leaning toward the latter. An e-mail whipping around the Web has the subject line "Sign on Wall St. yesterday," and shows a hand-lettered cardboard sign saying, "JUMP! You Fuckers!"

The *Manifesto* makes for quaint reading today. All that talk about "production," for example: Did they actually make things in those days? Did the proletariat really slave away in factories instead of call centers? But on one point Marx and Engels proved right: Within capitalist societies, or at least those with the kind of wildly unregulated capital-ism America has had, the rich got richer, the workers got poorer, and the erstwhile middle class has been sliding toward ruin. The last two outcomes are what Marx called "immiseration," which, in translation, is the process you're undergoing when you have cancer and no health insurance, or a mortgage payment due and no paycheck coming in.

Marx predicted that capitalism would fall in a spirited, proactive fashion: The workers, fed up with immiseration, would revolt, seize the "means of production," and insist on running the show themselves, that being the original, pre-Soviet notion of socialism. The revolution didn't happen, of course, at least not here. For the last several years, American workers have sweetly acquiesced to declining wages, rising prices, speedups at work, disappearing pensions, and increasingly threadbare health insurance. While CEO pay escalated to the eight-figure range and above, so-called ordinary Americans took on second jobs and moved in with relatives, where they faced uncomfortably long waits for the bathroom.

But all this immiseration—combined with fabulous enrichment at the top—did end up destabilizing the capitalist system, if only because, in the last few years, legions of Americans depended on easy credit to make up for inadequate wages. Until about a year ago, we got messages almost daily, by telemarketer and by mail, urging us to consolidate our debts, refinance our homes, transfer our debts from one credit card to another, and try tasty new mortgages that didn't even require a down payment. All too often, we bit. It sounded so reasonable, for example, not to let our assets just "sit" in our houses, but to start spending that money now.

At the other, Learjet end of the economic spectrum, there was the problem of what to do with too *much* money. Yes, this can be a problem. Some of the superrich have to hire consultants to help them spend their money: Where *do* you get a $20,000 bottle of wine, or find a Picasso for the bathroom wall? More seriously, there was the problem of what to invest in. As Chuck Collins of the Working Group on Extreme Inequality has pointed out, huge concentrations of wealth can function like rogue waves, smashing around recklessly in their search for ever-higher returns. A lot of these money waves flowed, directly or indirectly, into the dodgy credit schemes that were engulfing the un-rich majority, leaving even the fat cats imperiled by the toxic debts of the subprime class.

Marx's argument was that the coexistence of great wealth for the few and growing poverty for the many is not only morally objectionable, but also inherently unstable. He may have been wrong about the reasons for the instability, but no one can any longer deny it's there. When the greed of the rich collided with the needs of the poor—for a home, for example—the result was a global credit meltdown.

Obviously, the way to address the crisis is to deal with the poverty and inequality that led to it: bail out people facing foreclosures, make a massive, job-generating public investment in infrastructure, both physical and social, and, since medical debts are the number one cause of personal bankruptcy, enact universal health insurance immediately. But not even Obama, whose lawn sign I proudly displayed, seems to have the stomach for such a "trickle upwards" approach. During the final weeks of his campaign, he announced that he wouldn't bother taking the bailout as an opportunity to change the bankruptcy law so that people facing foreclosure can renegotiate their mortgages.

So happy birthday, *Communist Manifesto*—although I'm hoping that capitalism survives this one, if only because there's no alternative ready at hand. At the very least, we should get some regulation and serious oversight out of any bailout deal, meaning that, yes, the economy will look a little less like "free enterprise." But one thing we should have learned by now is that, when applied to enterprise, "freedom" can be just another word for someone else's pain.

MEANNESS

ON THE RISE

Pension or Penitentiary?

TALK ABOUT A CRY FOR HELP. ON MAY 1, 2006, TIMO-thy J. Bowers robbed a Columbus, Ohio, bank of $80, handed the money over to a security guard, and waited for the police to come and arrest him. In court, he pleaded guilty and told the judge that he would like a three-year sentence—just enough time to get him to the age of eligibility for Social Security benefits. The judge graciously obliged, demonstrating compassionate conservativism at its warmhearted best.

Bowers, almost sixty-five years old, is no wacko. He passed a court-ordered psychological exam and explained that he had not been able to find a new job since his old one ended when his employer's company closed in 2003. "At my age," he said, "the jobs available to me are minimum-wage jobs," adding that "there is age discrimination out there."

Bowers had hit a "doughnut hole" like the one that plagues Medicare recipients: he was "too old" for the above-minimum-wage workforce and too young for Social Security.

Given the labor market's fixation on youth, too old can mean as young as forty-five and a twenty-year gap before Social Security kicks in.

Leaving aside the obvious disadvantages of incarceration–having to pee in public, eat gross institutional food, etc.–Bowers made a perfectly rational choice. The minimum wage in Ohio is $5.15 an hour, or $824 a month before taxes, which won't get you much of a dwelling space in Columbus, at least not if you intend to maintain a regular schedule of meals. Prison, on the other hand, offers a free bed, free food, and, however inadequate, free health care. We can expect a rash of similar bank robberies as the middle-aged seek ways to wait out the years between the onset of age discrimination and the arrival of their first Social Security check.

There's nothing new about using prison as a solution to poverty. Over 2 million Americans are presently incarcerated, the great majority of them from the lowest income brackets. In fact, incarceration is expanding as the welfare state shrinks: While the United States offers 2 million prison beds, it provides public housing to only 1.3 million households, and that number is dropping rapidly. Bowers could have applied for a Section 8 housing voucher, but the waiting list for one exceeds, in some cities, his three-year prison term.

In short, we are reaching the point, if we have not passed it already, where the largest public housing program in America will be our penitentiary system.

If Bowers's choice was rational, the same cannot be said of our social policies. The cost of incarcerating an older inmate is about $69,000 a year. A compassionate–or merely rational–state would give Bowers a stipend to live on and save its prison beds for actual bad guys.

Where the Finger's Pointing

I'VE LOST MY APPETITE FOR WENDY'S CHILI, AND NOT because I'm afraid of finding a finger in it. When the finger-in-the-chili story first emerged, I was one of those loyal customers who placed their chili orders with a cheery request to "hold the finger, please." After all, the original bean-encrusted digit had been placed in the chili by the customer who found it, for the alleged purpose of suing Wendy's big-time. No, what's soured me on Wendy's is the sentence meted out to the finger planters—Anna Ayala and Jaime Placencia of Santa Clara, California—who have been found guilty of fraud and extortion and are being sent away for nine and twelve years respectively.

All right, it was a stupid trick, but an average of over ten years each? I could see three *months,* possibly six, for the temporary damage to the company's reputation. But no one should get ten years unless he or she is found guilty of putting two hands' worth of fingers into the chili—fingers that had been forcibly removed from the hands of Wendy's managers.

Asked to comment on the sentence, Placencia's lawyer said, "It certainly sends a clear and loud message." But what is the message—that American sentencing is out of control? Crimes that would get you a few months in a European court can put you away here for years. Under California's three-strikes-and-you're-out law, people have received life sentences for stealing a doughnut or slice of pizza. Excessive sentencing, combined with the war on drugs, has given the United States the unpleasant distinction of having the highest incarceration rate in the world.

There's another message here, too: Don't mess with a big corporation. If Ayala and Placencia had tried finger fraud at, say, Tony's Diner, they wouldn't have ended up owing anyone $21 million, the amount Wendy's claims to have lost in sales as a result of the fake finger food.

And if corporate power isn't one of the issues here, how come there's so little interest in the source of the finger? Placencia got it from an acquaintance named Brian Paul Rossiter, who has said it was severed in an "industrial accident" at the asphalt plant where he works. What kind of an accident? And how much was Rossiter's employer to blame? No one has taken the trouble to investigate, although the most grisly crime here—the human damage as opposed to the monetary loss—may have been the mutilation of this man's hand.

When a corporation is planting the fingers, the courts aren't likely to be anywhere near as vindictive as they were with Ayala and Placencia. Consider the case of Felipe Rocha, a California prison inmate who found a finger in his vegetarian meal. The finger turned out to have originated in another industrial accident—at a company called G.A. Food Services Inc., which supplies frozen meals to the prison. Freaked out by the unwanted protein supplement, Rocha sued the company for $75,000 but has so far been offered a settlement that, according to his lawyer, he considers "insultingly low." Again, no one seems to be alarmed over the "industrial accident" that nearly compromised Rocha's vegetarianism. Fingers are severed routinely in workplaces, and no one much notices till they land on a plate.

So I'm looking at my Wendy's chili a little more warily these days. The beans are recognizable, though I cannot be sure they are not the kidneys of a very small animal. It's the "meat" that worries me. Nothing I have ever done to beef in my kitchen has ever produced such perfect little pellets. But if I were to go into a Wendy's and point out, loudly, their remarkable resemblance to rodent turds, would I risk ending up like Rocha—and possibly now Ayala and Placencia—condemned to eat human fingers along with my prison chow while serving a multiyear term?

Things could be a lot worse, sentencingwise. *Harper's* magazine reports that the mayor of Las Vegas has proposed "thumbing" as a punishment for graffiti artists: "I'm saying that maybe you put them on TV and cut off a thumb." Brilliant solution, Mr. Mayor, only why not make them eat it, too?

The Cheapskate Warfare State

EVER WILLING TO "SUPPORT OUR TROOPS," WASHING-ton has come up with a new way to ease the burden on US soldiers: As a result of the 2008 farm bill, the extra pay the troops receive for serving in combat zones—$225 a month—will be permanently exempted from counting against their food stamp eligibility. This should bring true peace of mind to our men and women on the front lines. From now on, they can dodge bullets in Iraq with the happy assurance that their loved ones will not starve as a result of their bravery.

Military families on food stamps? It's not an urban myth. There are no hard statistics, and most service people don't qualify because of their military housing allowances. But many are eligible for another antipoverty program, the earned income tax credit, and Senator Harry Reid, Demo-crat of Nevada, reports hearing from constituents that the army now includes applications for food stamps in its orien-tation packet for new recruits.

The poverty of the mightiest military machine on earth is no secret to the many charities that have sprung up to help families on US military bases, like the church-based Feed the Children, which delivers free food and personal items to families at twelve bases. Before 9/11, trucks bearing free food from a variety of food pantries used to be able to drive right onto the bases. Now they have to stop outside the gates, making the spectacle of military poverty visible to any passerby. CBS has reported that a food bank near the Miramar Marine Air Station in the San Diego area serves five hundred military families a month.

Market forces ensure that a volunteer army will necessarily be an army of the poor. The trouble is, enlistment does not do a whole lot to brighten one's economic outlook. Frontline battle troops, most of whom have been in the military for about a year, earn about $17,000 a year—which puts them at about the level of theater ushers and crossing guards. Even second lieutenants, at a starting salary of $26,000 a year, earn less than pest control workers and shoe repairers. So when the Bush administration, in its frenzied rush to transfer more wealth to the already wealthy, squeezes the working poor, you can count the troops among them. The 2003 Bush tax cut for the rich, for example, failed to extend a child tax credit to nearly 200,000 military personnel.

Well, they get all kinds of special benefits, don't they, like free housing and medical care? Yes, and that's a powerful attraction to the young men and women of America's working poor. But no one should confuse the US military with a Swedish-style welfare state. The mother of a marine reports that her son had to charge nearly $1,000 on her Visa card for items not issued by the military, like camouflage paint and socks. In 2003, Defense Department overseas schools for the children of military personnel sometimes had to close a week early due to a lack of funds.

But it's not all bad news: The military death benefit received by families of the fallen has been raised from $12,000 to $250,000. That's a tempting sum. It may make death financially preferable to surviving in a damaged state. Bizarrely enough, veterans' disability benefits are deducted from their military retirement pay, giving the wounded a powerful incentive to die while they're young. The sorry condition of VA health services seems designed to accomplish the same thing, and those services may get a lot more inaccessible. The administration has proposed to raise veterans' health care costs—through increased drug copayments and a new "enrollment fee"—thus driving an estimated 200,000 vets out of the system and discouraging another million from enrolling.

In the interests of maintaining a calm and dispassionate tone here, let's not talk about the morality of sending the poor to distant countries to die for undisclosed reasons while nickel-and-diming them every inch of the way. It will suffice to point out what a peculiar historical anomaly Bush's warfare state represents. Ever since the introduction of mass armies in Europe in the seventeenth century, governments have generally understood that to underpay and underfeed one's troops is to risk having the guns pointed in the opposite direction from that which the officers are recommending. Modern welfare states, limited as they may be, are in no small part the product of war—that is, of governments' attempts to appease the warriors and the class of people that supplies them.

In this country, for example, the Civil War led to the institution of widows' benefits, which were the predecessor of welfare in its Aid to Families with Dependent Children form. The Prussian leader Bismarck, who was under pressure from socialists as well as the exigencies of war, instituted national health insurance. In the United States, World War II spawned educational benefits and income support for veterans. In the United Kingdom, it generated a far more generous welfare state than we have here, including free health care for all. Hitler built up a welfare state, too, including support for single women willing to produce fresh cannon fodder for his state of permanent war.

This has been the way of the world: If you want the working class to die for you, then you have to give it something in return.

Or perhaps there's a plan afoot to restock the US military with illegal immigrants, for whom $17,000 a year might look like a living wage?

If supporting our troops is to mean something more than a bumper sticker, the least we could do is lift them out of poverty.

Are Illegal Immigrants
the Problem?

I'VE BEEN READING WITH MIXED FEELINGS AN EXCHANGE on my Web site's forum on the subject of illegal immigration. One contributor writes that "the first step is to deport the illegal aliens and those overstaying their visas. This should open up millions of jobs." He—well, he says he's a male in his midthirties—must have been watching Lou Dobbs's strident series on "Our Broken Borders," which blames about 51 percent of our economic woes on illegal immigrants. Though to give Dobbs his due, he does pin the other 49 percent on "big corporations."

I've traveled across the US-Mexican border, and it didn't seem too broken to me. Peer through the giant fence that runs right to the Pacific Ocean in Tijuana and you see what looks like an armed encampment: That's America, the "land of opportunity," as viewed from the poorer parts of the world. On the way back north, it took fifty minutes to make our way through the US border checkpoint, waiting in bumper-to-bumper traffic as gaunt peddlers, many carrying babies on their backs, went from car to car selling trinkets and snacks.

The amazing thing is that so many Mexicans (and other Latin Americans) risk the border crossing and the hostile culture of the United States—a fact you're reminded of as soon as you enter California and see the first "human crossing" warning signs. These show a silhouetted family running together, reminding you that it's parents and children, not deer, you're likely to collide with just north of the fence.

Now we've been given a glimpse into the lives of one of the biggest categories of illegal Latino immigrants, the day laborers who do jobs like construction, moving, and landscaping. According to a 2006 study carried out by researchers at three major US universities, about three-fourths of the day laborers in this country lack legal documents. Not surprisingly, they live miserably. Their median earnings are $700 a month, most have no access to health care, and half of them said they'd been stiffed by bosses at one time or another and gone unpaid for their work.

That's what makes undocumented workers so attractive to unscrupulous US employers: When you rip them off, they have no recourse at all. So my first, knee-jerk response to Lou Dobbs et al. would be: If you don't want undocumented immigrants competing with Americans for jobs, stop the *exploitation* of the immigrants and make sure they work under the same laws and regulations as anyone else.

The real surprise in the study is that 49 percent of the day laborers interviewed said they were usually hired not by contractors or companies of any kind, and certainly not "big corporations," but by American homeowners. I'd heard Bay Buchanan (sister of Pat) on Lou Dobbs's show fulminating about the "big corporations" that are hiring all the illegal immigrants, but in fact it's the guy next door who needs his house painted or his lawn mowed.

So there's a sickening level of hypocrisy here. In the last few years, we've seen anti-immigrant protests at day laborer hiring sites—street corners or, very often, Home Depot parking lots—from Burbank, California, to Suffolk County, Long Island. But how many of those righteous protestors have employed undocumented immigrants themselves, if not as construction and lawn workers, then as nannies or maids?

But I do agree with one forum contributor when he writes: "I get very tired of ivory tower 'professional' types who dismiss the impact of these workers because they're just doing 'jobs nobody else wants to do.'" There's Jimmy, for example, a friend from Buffalo who hasn't had steady employment since he was laid off from an auto plant in the nineties. Now he's getting ready to move to South Florida, where there's still a shortage of workers to repair hurricane damage. His plan? Get a job, or at least hang out, at Home Depot, where the pay is low and the possibilities of advancement are negligible—so he might be spotted by potential employers.

With the catastrophic ongoing layoffs in the auto industry, we can expect more American citizens to join the immigrants congregating in Home Depot parking lots. They'll have a choice: to treat the immigrants as competitors and enemies or to band together with them, as coworkers, to fight for better wages and working conditions for all.

Of course, I hope they'll choose the latter. One image haunts me from my border crossing: a thin brown man in tattered clothes trying to sell handmade wooden crosses to the Americans crawling along in their cars. He was carrying one of the larger ones on his back.

The Shame Game

I WAS ON A RADIO CALL-IN SHOW IN MINNEAPOLIS NOT long ago, listening to the callers tell their tales of economic woe: an eight-month job search followed by a job at half the person's former pay, an eighteen-month search leading to serious depression, a five-year search leading to nothing at all. During a commercial break, my host noted that almost all these stories were told in the third person, usually as something that had happened to a spouse. Were some of the callers just too embarrassed to own their own stories—too crushed by the shame of layoffs and unemployment?

Shame hangs heavy over the economic landscape: the shame of the newly laid off, the shame of the chronically poor. It's easy enough for enlightened members of the comfortable classes to insist there's no reason for shame. *You* didn't bring the layoff down on yourself; *you* didn't determine that the maximum wage in your line of work would be in the neighborhood of $8 an hour. Snap out of it, I want to say, blame the economy or its corporate chieftains. Just don't blame yourself!

But shame is a verb as well as a noun. Almost nobody arrives at shame on their own; there are *shamers* and *shamees*. Hester Prynne didn't pin that scarlet A on her own chest. In fact, it may be wiser to think of shame as a relationship rather than just a feeling—a relationship of domination in which the mocking judgments of the dominant are internalized by the dominated.

Shaming can be a more effective means of social control than force. The peasant who stepped out of line could be derided for daring to question his betters. The woman who spoke out against patriarchal restrictions could be dismissed as a harridan or even a slut. It doesn't always work, of course. In 1994, Dan Quayle and right-wing writer Charles Murray launched an initiative to "restigmatize" out-of-wedlock births by restoring the old pejorative term *illegitimate*. But somehow the country wasn't ready to label millions of babies bastards.

Shame was far more effective in the buildup to welfare reform. Consistently stereotyped as lazy, promiscuous parasites, welfare recipients largely failed to rally in their own defense. I remember talking to a young (white) woman who professed great enthusiasm for draconian forms of welfare reform—only to admit that she herself had been raised on welfare by a beloved and plucky single mother. That's deeply internalized shame.

The ultimate trick is to make people ashamed of the injuries inflicted upon them. In many cultures, rape renders a woman an unmarriageable pariah. In Pakistan—one of our more embarrassing allies—a woman who brings charges of rape can be punished for "adultery." In 2007, a nineteen-year-old Saudi woman was sentenced to two hundred lashes for bringing charges of gang rape, until international pressure forced the Saudi king to "pardon" her. Even in America, many women's first response to sexual harassment or assault is to feel soiled and shamed, as if she had brought the unwanted advances on herself.

Something similar goes on in the case of the laid off and unemployed, thanks to the prevailing Calvinist form of Protestantism, according to which productivity and employment are the source of one's identity as well as one's income. Not working? Then what are you? And to put the Calvinist message in crude theological terms: *Go to hell.*

For those who fail to feel their full measure of shame over unemployment, there is an entire shame industry to whip them into shape: the career coaches, self-help books, motivational speakers, and business gurus who preach that whatever happens to you must be a result of your own "attitude." Laid off and coming up empty on your job search? You must be too "negative" and hence attracting negative circumstances into your life. To paraphrase one career coach I've heard: We're not here to talk about the economy or the market; we're here to talk about *you.*

Shame is a potent weapon, but it should never be used against the already injured and aggrieved. Instead, let's turn it against the aggrievers: Shame on Ford and GM for putting all their eggs in the SUV basket and then laying off thousands. Shame on the CEOs who make eight-figure incomes while their lowest-paid employees trudge between food banks. Shame on Congress for leaving us with an unemployment insurance program that covers only a little more than a third of the laid off.

Everyone else should hold their heads up high.

The New Cosby Kids

I T WAS SUCH A DOG-BITES-MAN STORY THAT I ALMOST skipped right by: Billionaire Bashes Poor Blacks. The only thing that gave this particular story a little piquancy is that the billionaire doing the bashing is black himself. Bill Cosby has been attacking the poor of his race, and especially the youthful poor, for a range of sins, including using bad words, "stealing pound cake," "giggling," and failing to give their children normal names like Bill. "The lower-economic people," Cosby has announced, "are not holding up their end in this deal."

They let me down, too, sometimes—like that girl at Wendy's who gave me sweet iced tea when I had clearly specified unsweetened. She looked a little tired, but, as Cos might point out, how hard can it be to hold a job, go to high school, and care for younger siblings in all your spare moments while your parents are at work?

Cos might not have noticed, but it's just so 1990s to beat up on the black poor. In anticipation of welfare reform in

1996, the comfortable denizens of think spas like the Heritage Foundation routinely excoriated poor black women for being government-dependent baby machines, not to mention overweight (that pound cake again). As for poor black youth, they were targeted in the nineties as a generation of "superpredators," gang bangers, and thugs.

It's time to start picking on a more up-to-date pariah group for the twenty-first century, and I'd like to nominate the elderly whites. Filial restraint has so far kept the would-be Social Security privatizers on the right from going after them, but the grounds for doing so are clear. For one thing, there's a startling new wave of "grandpa bandits" terrorizing rural banks. And occasionally some old duffer works himself into a frenzy listening to Cole Porter tunes and drives straight into a crowd of younger folks.

The law-abiding old whites are no prize either. Overwhelmingly, they choose indolence over employment— lounging on park benches, playing canasta—when we all know there are plenty of people-greeter jobs out there. Since it's government money that allows them to live in this degenerate state, we can expect the Heritage Foundation to reveal any day now that some seniors are cashing in their Social Security checks for vodka and Viagra. Just as welfare was said to "cause poverty," the experts may soon announce that Medicare causes baldness and that Social Security is a risk factor for osteoporosis: the correlations are undeniable.

And the menace posed by the elderly can only get worse, as ever more of them sink into debt. What's eating up their nest eggs? In many cases, drugs. How long before the streets are ruled by geezer gangs mugging us to support their insulin and beta-blocker habits?

All right, before the AARP issues a fatwa against me, could we please acknowledge that the demonization of the black youth who so exercise Cosby is not based on reality either: their pregnancy rates aren't "soaring," as he reportedly claimed; ditto with crime rates. And if Cosby's worried about poor grammar and so forth, why isn't he ranting about the savaging of a slew of programs for dropout prevention, recreation, and school counseling?

Or, if he's looking for tantrum fodder, what about the fact that a black baby has a 40 percent chance of being born into poverty? You can blame adults for their poverty—if you're mean-spirited enough—but you cannot blame babies, and that's, in effect, what we're talking about here.

As the sociologist Michael Males, who monitors youth-bashing outbreaks, told me: "Younger black America today is struggling admirably against massive disinvestments in schools, terrible unemployment, harsh policing, and degrading prejudices, and they're succeeding amazingly well. They deserve respect, not grown-up tantrums."

But it must be fun to beat up on people too young and too poor to fight back, or the elderly rich wouldn't do it. Cranky old rich people: now there's a demographic group that qualifies as a genuine Menace 2 Society.

What America Owes
Its "Illegals"

WHEN CONGRESS PROPOSED TO FINE UNDOCUMENTED immigrants $5,000 before they could seek citizenship, Rush Limbaugh expected liberals to start "whining" about the fine. But most liberals were too busy chortling about the immigration-induced split in the GOP to make their own case against the bill. So let a mighty whine rise up from the land: Undocumented workers shouldn't be fined; they should get a hefty bonus!

All right, they committed a "crime"—the international equivalent of breaking and entry. But breaking and entry is usually a prelude to a much worse crime, like robbery or rape. What have the immigrants been doing once they get into the United States? Taking up time on the elliptical trainers in our health clubs? Getting ahead of us on the wait lists for elite private nursery schools?

In case you don't know what immigrants do in this country, the Latinos have a word for it—*trabajo*. They've been mowing the lawns, cleaning the offices, hammering the nails, and picking the tomatoes, not to mention all that dishwashing, diaper changing, meatpacking, and poultry plucking.

The punitive rage directed at illegal immigrants grows out of a larger blindness to the manual labor that makes our lives possible: the touching belief, in the class occupied by Rush Limbaugh among many others, that offices clean themselves at night and salad greens spring straight from the soil onto one's plate.

Native-born workers share in this invisibility, but it's far worse in the case of immigrant workers, who are often, for all practical purposes, nameless. In the recent book *There's No José Here: Following the Lives of Mexican Immigrants*, Gabriel Thompson cites a construction company manager who says things like, "I've got to get myself a couple of Josés for this job if we're going to have that roof patched up by Saturday." Forget the Juans, Diegos, and Eduardos—they're all interchangeable Josés.

Hence no doubt the ease with which some prominent immigrant bashers forget their own personal reliance on immigrant labor, like Governor Jim Gibbons of Nevada, who, it turns out, once employed an undocumented nanny. And as the *Boston Globe* revealed late last year, Mitt Romney's lawn in suburban Boston was maintained by illegal immigrants from Guatemala.

The only question is how *much* we owe our undocumented immigrant workers. First, those who do not remain to enjoy the benefits of old age in America will have to be reimbursed for their contributions to Medicare and Social Security, and here I quote the Web site of the San Diego ACLU: "Undocumented immigrants annually pay an estimated $7 billion more than they take out into Social Security, and $1.5 billion more into Medicare. . . . A study by the

National Academy of Sciences also found that tax payments generated by immigrants outweighed any costs associated with services used by immigrants."

Second, someone is going to have to calculate what is owed to "illegals" for wages withheld by unscrupulous employers like the homeowner who tells his or her domestic worker that the wage is actually several hundred dollars a month less than she had been promised and that the home-owner will be "holding" it for her. Or the landscaping service that stiffs its undocumented workers for their labor. Who's the "illegal" here?

Third, there's the massive compensation owed to undoc-umented immigrants for preventable injuries on the job. In her book *Suburban Sweatshops: The Fight for Immigrant Rights*, Jennifer Gordon reports such gruesome cases as a Hon-duran who died from inhaling paint while sanding yachts on Long Island and a Guatemalan worker whose boss in-tentionally burned him with hot pans of oil for not washing dishes fast enough. "Death rates for Latino workers," Gor-don reports, "have risen over the past decade even as work-place fatality rates for non-Latinos have fallen."

When our debt to America's undocumented workers is eventually tallied, I'm confident that it will be well in excess of the $5,000 fine the immigration bill proposed. There is still the issue of the original "crime." If someone breaks into my property for the purpose of trashing and looting, I would be hell-bent on restitution. But if they break in for the purpose of cleaning it—scrubbing the bathroom, mow-ing the lawn—then, in my way of thinking anyway, the debt goes in the other direction.

The Suicide Solution

W HILE CONGRESS WAS DEBATING HOW TO HELP distressed homeowners, Carlene Balderrama of Taunton, Massachusetts, found her own solution to the mortgage crisis. Just a little over two hours before her mortgage company, PHH Mortgage Corporation—may its name live in infamy—was to auction off her home, Balderrama killed herself with her husband's rifle.

This is not the kind of response to hard times that James Grant had in mind when he wrote a *Wall Street Journal* essay entitled "Why No Outrage?" "One might infer from the lack of popular anger," the famed Wall Street contrarian wrote, "that the credit crisis was God's fault rather than the doing of the bankers and the rating agencies and the government's snoozing watchdogs." For contrast, he cites the spirited response to the depression of the 1890s, when lawyer and agitator Mary Lease stirred crowds by saying, "We want the accursed foreclosure system wiped out. . . .

We will stand by our homes and stay by our firesides by force if necessary."

Grant could have found even more bracing examples of resistance in the 1930s, when farmers and tenants used mob power—and sometimes firearms—to fight foreclosures and evictions. For more on that, I consulted Frances Fox Piven, coauthor of the classic text *Poor People's Movements: Why They Succeed, How They Fail,* who told me that in the early '30s, a number of cities were so shaken by the resistance that they declared moratoriums on further evictions. A 1931 riot by Chicago tenants who had fallen behind on their rent, for example, had left three dead and three police officers injured.

According to Piven, these actions were often spontaneous. A group of unemployed men would get word of a scheduled eviction and march through the streets, gathering crowds as they went. Arriving at the site of the eviction, they would move the furniture back into the apartment and stay around to protect the threatened tenants. In one instance in Detroit, it took one hundred cops to evict a single family. Also in Detroit, Piven said, "two families protected their apartments by shooting their landlord and were acquitted by a sympathetic jury."

What a difference eighty years makes. When the police and the auctioneers arrived at Balderrama's house, the family gun had already been used—on the victim of foreclosure herself. I don't know how "worthy" a debtor she was—the family had been through bankruptcies before, though probably not as a result of Caribbean vacations and closets full of designer clothes. It was an adjustable rate mortgage that did them in, and Balderrama, who managed the family's finances, had apparently been unwilling to tell her husband that their ever-rising monthly mortgage payments were eating up his earnings as a plumber.

Suicide is becoming an increasingly popular response to debt. James Scurlock's brilliant documentary, *Maxed Out*, features the families of two college students who killed themselves after being overwhelmed by credit card debt. "All the people we talked to had considered suicide at least once," Scurlock told a gathering of the National Association of Consumer Bankruptcy Attorneys in 2007. According to the *Los Angeles Times*, lawyers in the audience backed him up, "describing clients who showed up at their offices with cyanide, or threatened, 'If you don't help me, I've got a gun in my car.'"

Reporter Nick Turse has been compiling a list of economically motivated suicides like Balderrama's. In October '08, Karthik Rajaram of Los Angeles killed his wife, his three sons, and his mother-in-law before shooting himself, explaining in a note that he had incurred massive losses in the economic meltdown. Similarly, a Florida man facing foreclosure shot his wife and his dog, set fire to his house, then killed himself. When a Colorado sheriff's deputy went to serve an eviction notice, he found that the homeowner had slashed his wrists and was lying in a pool of blood.

India may be the trendsetter here. An estimated 150,000 debt-ridden Indian farmers have succumbed to suicide since 1997. With guns in short supply in rural India, the desperate farmers have taken to drinking the pesticides meant for their crops.

Dry your eyes, already: Death *is* an effective remedy for debt, along with anything else that may be bothering you. And try to think of it too from a lofty, corner-office perspective: If you can't pay your debts or afford to play your role as a consumer, and if, in addition—like an ever-rising number of Americans—you're no longer needed at the workplace, then there's no further point to your existence. I'm not saying that the creditors, the bankers, and the mortgage companies actually *want* you dead, but in a culture where one's credit rating is routinely held up as a three-digit measure of personal self-worth, the correct response to insoluble debt is in fact, "Just shoot me!"

The alternative is to value yourself more than any amount of money, and turn the guns, metaphorically speaking, in the other direction. It wasn't God, or some abstract economic climate change, that caused the credit crisis. Actual humans—often masked as financial institutions—did that. Most of them, except for a tiny few facing trials, are still high rollers, fattening themselves on the blood and tears of ordinary debtors. I know it's so 1930s, but may I suggest a march on Wall Street?

STRANGLING THE MIDDLE CLASS

UCD WOMEN'S CENTER

Freshpersons, Welcome to Debt!

WELCOME TO FLEECE U, WHERE OUR MISSION IS TO take feckless teenagers such as yourselves and turn them into full-fledged citizens of our economy, meaning, of course, debtors.

Many life-changing things will happen to you in the next four years. You will make lasting friends, including perhaps the love of your life. You will drink more than you ever thought possible and bitterly regret it in the morning. You will lose your virginity, if you happen to have brought it with you.

Our stellar faculty ardently hopes that along the way you will be amazed by calculus and charmed by the tipsy conversation between Alcibiades and that wily old radical Socrates. There is also a general expectation that you will come out of here with some hazy notions of spelling and grammar.

But never forget that your real purpose is to shake off the pointless freedom of youth and assume the burden of debt.

To this end, we have just raised our tuition in an attempt to keep up with such top-of-the-line institutions as George Washington University (now weighing in at $39,210 a year, or $50,000 with room and board). You will find us also charging a plethora of additional fees—a "student activities fee," a "technology fee," and an "incidentals fee." In addition, we will be experimenting this year with a "snow removal fee," a "lecture hall seat-use fee," and the installation of pay toilets in the dorms.

It would be shortsighted to resent these fees, since they provide valuable experience in bill reading and will come in handy when you confront your own personal monthly utility statements. At present we do not charge any additional tuition for this training in bill reading, though we are considering adding a special "fee fee" in the future.

Another thing that will help ease you into the status of debtor is the price of your textbooks—about $120 to $180 for a new, graffiti-free copy. True, this seems high when you could buy a hardcover of *Harry Potter and the Deathly Hallows* for $20 or less, but the aim is to teach you that a book is something to treasure (and, again, we charge no extra fee for this lesson).

On average, you will graduate with a respectable-sized debt of $20,000, which will enable you to establish your all-important "credit history." If we have succeeded in our educational mission, you will be a first-rate debtor, capable of making minimum monthly payments much of the time. As fresh offers of credit cards and home equity loans pour in, you will beam with pride at your achievement.

Please note carefully that a Fleece U degree cannot guarantee you a future income that will allow you to pay off your debts. Many of our most promising graduates are now, three or four years later, working for $8–12 an hour serving up lattes, counseling disturbed youth, or creating business computer networks. They are set for a lifetime of debt, and we are proud that they first began to accrue it right here, on our lovely mock Oxfordian campus.

We don't have to remind you not to stigmatize debt as a condition associated with poverty. In 2006, for the first time, the average household's debt exceeded its income. By becoming a debtor, you will have entered the American mainstream! We have confidence that you will go on to mature effortlessly from college debt to car loan to mortgage to medical debts occasioned by the ever-growing gaps in coverage.

You will see the value of all this debt when the day comes, as it inevitably will, when you wake up and ask yourself, "Who am I and what am I doing here?" You will be tempted to take long walks, read the *Upanishads*, or try out for a new career as a trophy spouse.

In a crisis like this, you could easily spend thousands of dollars on life coaching and motivational DVDs. But you won't have to, because you'll have debt to keep you going. You will get up, shower, and toil faithfully in your cubicle year after year until, in the fullness of time, your family incurs debt to pay for your interment (at which point we trust you will have remembered Fleece U in your will).

So think of debt as the great motivator. Think of it as our *gift* to you. Because for at least the next academic year, we are not even thinking of charging for it.

Party On

WHAT IS SPRING WITHOUT THE TORMENT OF FOLDING chairs and long-winded platitudes involving the future and all the glories it holds? I've been to two college commencements in the space of three weeks—one where my nephew received his degree in computer networking and one at which I was given an honorary degree in "humane letters"—and I've seen the happy, uplifted young faces as well as those slightly blurred by drink. At UConn-Storrs, where I was honored, graduates enlivened the proceedings by bouncing large blow-up balls around the bleachers, to the consternation of the college president, who whispered to me, "This is the problem with having the commencement in the afternoon. Some of these people have been partying for hours."

There are reasons, whether the graduates know them or not, to want to greet one's entrance into the work world with an excess of Bud. At one point, back when I got my own real, nonhonorary BA in the sixties, a college degree was a more or less guaranteed ticket to the middle or upper middle class. With that diploma in hand, I could kiss my waitressing days good-bye. Today, no one even thinks of a college grad as being overqualified for tray carrying. In some urban restaurants, a degree almost seems to be required, if only so you can pronounce the day's specials.

According to my economics guru, Jared Bernstein at the Economic Policy Institute, there are about seven million college graduates working in jobs that do not require college degrees, and you can bet that most of them are not in high-end non-degree-requiring occupations like rap star or NFL quarterback. Furthermore, Bernstein says, the wage gap between the college educated and non–college educated is beginning to narrow, and not because the wages of the latter are rising.

Take my nephew, for example, who maintained a nearly 4.0 GPA and graduated with "highest distinction." He's seen a lot of job possibilities in the weeks since his graduation, but they all pay in the $8–9 an hour range, which is far less than he used to earn as a delivery truck driver. His brother-in-law, who is single and also college educated, has a weekday computer-related job that he supplements by working at a gas station on weekends. Similarly, my son followed up his Ivy League education with years of phone answering and fact-checking before joining me as one of the tiny number of self-supporting freelance writers who do not have the advantage of a trust fund.

It's too soon to call college a scam, and as long as colleges teach a few truly enlightening things, like history and number theory, I won't. But with tuition up between $10,000 and $50,000, the "return on investment" isn't looking that good. In fact, a BA may be worth about as much as my new "honorary doctorate": with these degrees and about $2, you can get a ride on a bus.

Looking at the thousands of happy—and in many cases, soon to be disappointed—young faces at the UConn graduation, I couldn't help wondering whether the real economic function of higher education isn't to keep the unemployment figures low. About 30 percent of young people in the 18–23-year-old age group are in college, so imagine what the unemployment rate would look like if they were all dumped into the workforce overnight. Maybe students are beginning to notice that college is becoming less of a stepping stone and more of a holding pen, and maybe that accounts for the rise in binge drinking and the alleged decline of intellectual curiosity. I don't know, but party on, graduates—this may be your last opportunity.

Fastest-Growing Jobs of '06:
Are You Handy with Bedpans
and Brooms?

URGENT BREAKING NEWS FOR ALL JOB-SEEKERS: THE Bureau of Labor Statistics has released a list of the fastest-growing jobs, and you might want to revise your résumé accordingly. I quickly scanned it to see if "dissident freelance blogger" was on the list, but, alas, no. Nor were several other job categories that I would like to see on the increase, like primary care physician and particle physicist. I'm sorry, but we're never going to get out of this nightmarish tangle of string theory and dark matter until we start generating huge cohorts of baby physicists.

Worse news—only ten of the twenty-five jobs listed pay over $30,000 a year, and four of them pay less than $20,000 a year, which is just about the poverty level for a family of four. These are waiter/waitress, food preparation worker, and home health aides. Hovering just a little bit above $20,000 are janitor, hand laborer, receptionist, nursing aide, landscaping worker, and teacher assistant. And topping the list as the fastest-growing job of all is retail salesperson at $22,880.

You see a pattern here? That's right, these are not the kinds of jobs you are hoping your brilliant, or at least above average, children will aspire to. In fact, the most shocking feature of the BLS list is that only five of these fastest-growing jobs require a college degree—or exactly 20 percent. OK, the third-fastest-growing job is "postsecondary teacher," but in a job market dominated by janitors, truck drivers, and customer service reps, what are these professors going to be teaching—"combination food preparation and serving"?

Now of course the fastest-growing jobs are not the only jobs available. There's still presumably a need for a few elevator operators, blacksmiths, and dissident freelance bloggers. But the list does give us a clue as to where our economy is headed, and it's not in the direction we were promised.

For decades now, the mantra has been "get an education and you'll be OK." In some ways it made sense: over the last twenty years, the earnings gap between college-educated and non-college-educated workers widened to the point where the educated had a 70 percent advantage. Even though that gap has begun to shrink a bit, a BA on your résumé remains almost as essential as an e-mail address.

At a certain point in the late 1990s and early 2000s, higher education was beginning to look like the solution to all our problems. Robert Reich touted it when he was Clinton's secretary of labor and, on the more conservative end of the spectrum, dozens of readers of *Nickel and Dimed* wrote to inform me that the problem with the working poor was that they just hadn't bothered to go to college. Outsourcing was no threat to the educated, according to this line of reasoning, since the United States would send the dumb, routine jobs abroad and keep the creative ones here. We would be a nation of thinkers and innovators, and the world would be our assembly line.

But that's not how it's turning out. Some companies have begun outsourcing their R & D—that is, their creativity and innovation. And when we study the list of fastest-growing jobs left here in the United States, we see a future filled with mops and trays, shovels and bedpans, and cash registers.

Don't let this stop you from going to college if you haven't already and you're lucky enough to have the money to do so. After all, we, or the science nuts among us anyway, need those particle physicists.

But you should consider revising your résumé to suit the demands of our new "new economy." Did you ever make lattes, rake leaves, or change diapers? Good, pump that up! And you might want to lose that MFA or PhD, because it would be a mistake to look "overqualified" for life in twenty-first-century America.

Your Local News—
Dateline Delhi

THE WORLD MAY BE FLAT, AS *NEW YORK TIMES* COLUM-nist Thomas Friedman has written, but I always liked to think I was standing on a bit of a hill. Now comes the news that pasadenanow.com, a local news site, is recruiting reporters in India. The Web site's editor points out that he can get two Indian reporters for a mere $20,800 a year—and no, they won't be commuting from New Delhi. Since Pasadena's city council meetings can be observed on the Web, the Indian reporters will be able to cover local politics from half the planet away. And if they ever feel a need to see the potholes of Pasadena, there's always Google Earth.

Excuse me, but isn't this more or less what former *New York Times* reporter Jayson Blair was fired for—pretending to report from sites around the country while he was actually holed up in his Brooklyn apartment? Or will pasadenanow.com be honest enough to give its new reporters datelines in Delhi (or wherever they live)?

I should have seen it coming. In the eighties, US

companies began outsourcing the manufacturing of everything from garments to steel, leaving whole cities to die.
Education was the recommended solution for the unemployed because in the globalized future Americans would
be the world's brains while Mexicans and Malaysians
would provide the hands.

So no one really complained when the back office and
call center jobs migrated to India in the nineties: who
needed them? We would still be the brains of global business. When the IT jobs started drifting away, we were at first
assured that only the more "routine" ones were outsource-
able. As for all the laid-off techies, they were smart enough
to develop new skills, right?

But no one can pretend any longer that we have a global
monopoly on intellect and innovation. Look at the
"telemedicine" trend, which has radiologists in India and
Lebanon reading CT scans for hospitals in Altoona and
Chicago. Or—and this was never supposed to happen—the
growing outsourcing of R & D, with scores of companies
opening labs in India or China—"Chindia," as they are
known in the biz lit. A Microsoft manager told the *Financial
Times* that "the question is how you make [the Chinese]
truly creative, truly innovative." Whoops—weren't we supposed to be the innovators?

Still, writing was believed to be safe, the last strong-
hold of Western creativity. Explaining the outsourcing of
almost every newspaper function, including copyediting,
the billionaire CEO of a consortium of Irish newspapers
wrote: "With the exception of the magic of writing and
editing news . . . almost every other function, except print-
ing, is location-indifferent." But the magic has clearly been
fading, starting three years ago when Reuters began outsourcing its Wall Street coverage to Bangalore. Is there

nothing an actual, on-site American can do better than anyone else?

In the Pasadena case, I can't even complain, as US-based Reuters workers did when their jobs were outsourced, that the quality of journalism will suffer as a result. One of the Indian reporters just hired by pasadenanow.com has a degree from the Graduate School of Journalism at UC Berkeley, which is one of the three or four best j-schools in the country. I have taught there myself and know that the students are scarily smart. Too bad that these reporters couldn't get real on-site journalism jobs, at normal American wages, but American newspapers are axing good journalists even as I write.

No, I don't resent the Indians for moving in on the kind of work I do. I just hope the next time some managers get the idea of cost saving through outsourcing they go for the CEO's job. That's where the big bucks are, and there's no reason to think a Chinese or Indian person couldn't do a CEO's work, whatever it may be, perfectly adequately, and at less than a tenth of the price. As for me, I'm retraining as a massage therapist, at least until they figure out how to do that from Mumbai.

That Sinking Feeling

D O YOU HAVE THAT SINKING FEELING? AS IN THE ROYAL Bank of Scotland's commercial where a fellow goes down in quicksand while his colleagues stand by, listening to their team leader's corpo-babble about the need to remain calm and develop a strategic multiphase plan to extricate the fellow who is rapidly disappearing into the muck? Well, it may be because you *are* sinking. As reported by the Federal Reserve, family incomes fell between 2001 and 2004 and remained below their 2000 peak at the end of 2006.

At first I hesitated to say anything about this, because *New York Times* columnist David Brooks has chided me personally for taking "an overly negative view of reality" and being out of touch with "the broader society." Perhaps I've been living in my own little miserable subculture where people struggle to make rent, sweat about threatened layoffs, and agonize over health insurance. Maybe I should get out more often.

But here it is—a bunch of bad news that even I couldn't

have seen coming. According to the Fed, average inflation-adjusted family incomes dropped by 2.3 percent between 2001 and 2004, to $70,700. The median family income (the point that half the families are above) rose only slightly, to $43,200, and the big difference between the median and average reflects how skewed the income distribution is.

Since 2000, it has become even more skewed, with—if you will pardon the all-too-familiar expression—the rich getting richer and the poor getting poorer. To quote the Associated Press: "The top 10 percent of households saw their net worth rise by 6.1 percent to an average of $3.11 million while the bottom 25 percent suffered a decline from a net worth in which their assets equaled their liabilities in 2001 to owing $1,400 more than their total assets in 2004."

Now if you can recall that distant period, this was a time of "recovery" from the bottoming out in 2001, with rising economic growth, productivity, and profits. So why did family incomes fall while other economic indicators rose? According to the Economic Policy Institute, the problem is that, whatever else is growing, wages are *not*. I'm no economist, but if the economy is growing and wages are not, the money must be going somewhere, and the obvious place to look is *up*.

Way up. In fact, if you want to follow the money you're going to have to strain your neck. Another *New York Times* columnist, economist Paul Krugman, reported on a study showing that those in the top 10 percent of the income distribution have been seeing income gains of only about 1 percent a year, or a total of 34 percent between 1972 and 2001. In that same period, those in the top 1 percent of the income distribution saw a gain of 87 percent, and those in the top .01 percent registered a gain of 497 percent. That's right: four hundred and ninety-seven percent.

Reading Krugman's column, I see I have been guilty of the opposite sin from that which Brooks accused me of—what he calls "the 80–20 fallacy." I'd been bright-siding the economy by assuming, as you may have as well, that the top 20 percent of the income distribution, which includes most college-educated workers, was doing fairly well. But the 2006 Economic Report of the President reveals that the real earnings of college graduates actually fell more than 5 percent between 2000 and 2004.

Could you *New York Times* guys please get together? I'm beginning to suffer from a little whiplash here.

But if you return to Brooks with a calculator in hand, you see there may be no inconsistency at all. Brooks cheerily reports that "only" 19 percent of American males and 27 percent of females are in poverty—a percentage that is "probably much smaller than most progressive commentators would estimate." If you average 19 and 27 percent, weighting for a 51 percent female population, you get an overall poverty rate of 23 percent. To my mind, a 23 percent poverty rate is totally outrageous, especially when compared with the federal government's faux poverty rate of about 12 percent. So are falling incomes for the college-educated middle class and mounting plunder for the plutocrats at the top. Maybe I've been living in the "broader society" after all.

What's So Great about
Gated Communities?

A NOTHER UTOPIA SEEMS TO BE BITING THE DUST. THE socialist kibbutzim of Israel have vanished or gone increasingly capitalist, and now the paranoid residential ideal represented by gated communities may be in serious trouble. Never exactly cool–remember Jim Carrey in *The Truman Show*?–these pricey enclaves of the white upper middle class are becoming hotbeds of disillusionment.

At the annual meeting of the American Anthropological Association in Washington in 2007, incoming association president Setha Low painted a picture so dispiriting that the audience guffawed in schadenfreude. The gated community residents Low interviewed had fled from ethnically challenging cities, but they have not managed to escape from their fear. One resident reported that her small daughter has developed a severe case of xenophobia, no doubt communicated by her parents: "We were driving next to a truck with some day laborers and equipment in the back, and we stopped beside them at the light. She [her daughter] wanted to move because she was afraid those people were going to come and get her. They looked scary to her."

Leaving aside the sorry spectacle of homeowners living in fear of their landscapers, there is actually something to worry about. According to Low, gated communities are no less crime-prone than open ones, and Gopal Ahluwalia, senior vice president of research at the National Association of Home Builders, confirms this: "There are studies indicating that there are no differences in the crime in gated communities and nongated communities." The security guards often wave people on in, especially if they look like they're on a legitimate mission—such as the faux moving truck that entered a Fort Meyers gated community last spring and left with a houseful of furniture. Or the crime comes from within, as at the Hilton Head Plantation community in South Carolina, where a rash of crime committed by resident teenagers has led to the imposition of a curfew.

Most recently, America's gated communities have been blighted by foreclosures. Yes, even people who were able to put together the down payment on a half-million-dollar house can be ambushed by adjustable rate mortgages and forced down from the upper to the lower middle class. *Newsweek* reports that foreclosures are devastating the gated community of Black Mountain Vista in Henderson, Nevada, where "yellow patches [now] blot the spartan lawns and phone books lie on front porches, their covers bleached from weeks under the desert sun." Similarly, according to the *Orlando Sentinel*, "countless homeowners overwhelmed by their mortgages are taking off and leaving behind algae-filled swimming pools and knee-high weeds" in one local gated community.

So for people who sought not just prosperity but perfection, here's another sad end to the American dream, or at least their ethnically cleansed version thereof: boarded-up McMansions, plastic baggies scudding over overgrown lawns, and, in the Orlando case, a foreclosure-induced infestation of snakes. You can turn away the Mexicans, the African Americans, the teenagers, and other suspect groups, but there's no fence high enough to keep out the repo man.

All right, some gated communities are doing better than others, and not all of their residents are racists. The communities that allow owners to rent out their houses or that offer homes at middle-class prices of $250,000 or so are more likely to contain a mixture of classes and races. The only gated community I have ever visited consisted of dull row houses protected by a slacker guard and a fence, and my host was a writer of modest means and liberal inclinations. But all these places suffer from the delusion that security lies behind physical barriers.

Before we turn all of America into a gated community, with a seven-hundred-mile steel fence running along the southern border, we should consider the mixed history of exclusionary walls. Ancient and medieval European towns huddled behind massive walls, only to face ever more effective catapults, battering rams, and other siege engines. More recently, the Berlin Wall, which the East German government described fondly as a protective "antifascism wall," fell to a rebellious citizenry. Israel, increasingly sealed behind its anti-Palestinian checkpoints and wall, faced an outbreak of neo-Nazi crime in September—coming, strangely enough, from within.

But the market may have the last word on America's internal gated communities. "Hell is a gated community," announced the *Sarasota Herald-Tribune* last June, reporting that market research by the big home builder Pulte Homes found that no one under fifty wants to live in them, so its latest local development would be ungated. Security, or at least the promise of security, may be one consideration. But there's another old-fashioned American imperative at work here, which ought to bear on our national policies as well. As my Montana forebears would have put it: *Don't fence me in!*

World's Designated
Shoppers Drop

How much lower can consumer spending go? The malls are like mausoleums, retail clerks are getting laid off, and AOL recently featured on its welcome page the story of a man so cheap he recycles his dental floss—hanging it from a nail in his garage until it dries out.

It could go a lot lower, of course. This guy could start saving the little morsels he flosses out and boiling them up to augment the children's breakfast gruel. Already, as the recession tightens its grip, people have stopped buying homes and cars and cut way back on restaurant meals. They don't have the money, they don't have the credit, and increasingly they're finding that no one wants their money anyway. NPR has reported that more and more Manhattan stores are accepting euros and at least one has gone euros-only.

The Sharper Image has declared bankruptcy and has closed all US retail stores. (To think I missed my chance to buy those headphones that treat you to forest sounds while massaging your temples!) Victoria's Secret is so desperate that it's adding fabric to its undergarments. Starbucks had no sooner taken time off to teach its baristas how to make coffee than it started laying them off.

While Americans search for interview outfits in consignment stores and switch from Whole Foods to Wal-Mart for sustenance, the world watches tremulously. The Australian newspaper *Courier-Mail*, for example, warns of an economic "pandemic" if Americans cut back any further, since we are responsible for $9 trillion a year in spending, compared to a puny $1 trillion for the one-billion-strong Chinese. Yes, we have been the world's designated shoppers, and if we fall down on the job, we take the global economy with us.

"Shop till you drop," was our motto, by which we didn't mean to say we were more compassion-worthy than a woman fainting at her workstation in some Honduran sweatshop. It was just our proper role in the scheme of things. Some people make stuff; other people have to buy it. And when we gave up making stuff, starting in the 1980s, we were left with the unique role of buying. Remember Bush telling us, shortly after 9/11, to get out there and shop? It may have seemed ludicrous at the time, but what he meant was *get back to work*.

We took pride in our role in the global economy. No doubt it takes some skill to make things, but what about all the craft that goes into buying them—finding a convenient parking space at the mall, navigating our way through department stores laid out for maximum consumer confusion, determining which of our credit cards still has a smidgeon of credit in it? Not everyone could do this, especially not people whose only experience was stitching, assembling, wiring, and packaging the stuff that we bought.

But if we thought we were special, they thought we were

marks. They could make anything, and we would dutifully buy it. I once found, in a party store, a baseball cap with a plastic turd affixed to its top and the words "shit head" on the visor. The label said "Made in the Philippines" and the workers must have been convulsed as they made it. *If those dumb Yanks will buy this . . .*

There's talk already of emergency measures, like making Christmas a weekly holiday, although this would require a level of deforestation that could leave Cheney with no quail to hunt.

More likely, there'll be a move to outsource shopping, just as we've already outsourced manufacturing, customer service, X-ray reading, and R & D. But to whom? The Indians are clever enough, but right now they only account for $600 million in consumer spending a year. And could they really be trusted to put a flat-screen TV in every child's room, distinguish Guess jeans from a knockoff, and replace their kitchen counters on an annual basis?

And what happens to us, the world's erstwhile shoppers? The president recently observed, in one of his more sentient moments, that unemployment is "painful." But if a pink slip hurts, what about a letter from Citicard announcing that you've been laid off as a shopper? Will we fill our vacant hours twisting recycled dental floss onto spools, or will we decide that if we can't shop, we're going to have to shop *lift*?

Because we've shopped till we dropped all right, face down on the floor.

HELL DAY
AT WORK

Circuit City Slaughter

CIRCUIT CITY CEO PHILIP J. SCHOONOVER IS ASSURED of getting a warm welcome in hell–very very warm. Columnist Bill White of the *Allentown Morning Call* imagines Satan telling him, "This place is full of overpaid, outsourcing, golden-parachuting, employee-abusing worms like you." Schoonover's sin? Laying off 3,400 employees because they had been around for too long and needed to be replaced by minimum-wage workers. His punishment? Having a choice of Dick Cheney or Nancy Grace as a roommate and spending eternity listening to Sanjaya's greatest hits.

The *New York Times* took the Circuit City slaughter with much greater equanimity. In his economics column, David Leonhardt showed some pious sympathy for the laid off, who will, after a ten-week cooling-off period, be able to reapply for their old jobs at much reduced pay. But he goes on to explain that Circuit City's employee abuse is just part of the larger corporate demand for "efficiency." Wal-Mart, after all, has capped employee pay and taken the stools away from its elderly employees. Sadly, Leonhardt observes: "It's probably not possible to halt these changes. It may not even be desirable. The flexibility of the American labor force seems to be one reason that recessions have been less frequent and unemployment less of a problem here than in Europe, notes Jason Furman, a leading Democratic economist."

Furman, by the way, is a pretty flexible guy himself. An adviser to John Kerry in 2004, then an NYU professor, and now a project director at a centrist think tank, he's made his mark as a "liberal" defender of Wal-Mart's antiworker policies. It's fellows like Furman who put the "ick" in the word *Democratic*.

But from Allentown to Times Square, no one is commenting on where the new flexibility may be taking us. Time was, not so long ago, when seniority was rewarded with higher pay and other perks. But that higher pay now carries a lethal risk. As a friend who writes software for a major multinational explained to me: "If you ask for a raise, the boss is going to say, 'Why would you want that? It would be like having a bull's-eye painted on your back.'" The more you make, the more tempting it is to fire you.

I experienced this myself a few years ago when I lost a lucrative writing contract with a major media outlet. "Why?" I asked my agent. "They said they were paying you more than any of their other outside writers," she told me, as if that were a sufficient explanation. Foolish me, I thought the raises I had gotten meant the bosses were pleased with my work. What they meant was that I was doomed.

Once you fire the high performers and experienced workers, the next step will be to demand that employees pay you for the privilege of working. Why not? Most workplaces provide air-conditioned environments and bathroom facilities, complete with soap and paper towels. These are things you'd expect to pay for in a hotel, so why should workers get them free? Having busted his $10–20-an-hour senior employees down to $8 and change an hour, Schoonover's bound to see that the best route to higher profit margins is negative pay.

I know what Schoonover's defense will be when he gets to the pearly gates: "The market made me do it." He'll be confident about getting into the Good Place, because for men like him, as well as Leonhardt and Furman, whom he'll bring along as character witnesses, the market is in fact the deity, determining who will starve and who will eat, who will work and who will beg.

But if the deity is someone other than "the market," if He or She turns out to be a moral entity, capable of distinguishing right from wrong, then poor Schoonover—it'll be Sanjaya for all eternity.

Blood in the Chutney

Genentech is sitting on the top of the world—well, actually, down in Silicon Valley. It has a $4 billion portfolio and is raking in cash from the high-profile anticancer agents Avastin and Herceptin. Thankful patients write all the time, and the company duly reprints their letters as full-page ads in places like the *New York Times*. "I am so grateful to the team that worked on the cancer medicine that I believe saved my life," reads a letter from former patient Joel Golub. "Your discovery has given me a chance to . . . go to a dance recital for my beautiful daughter, see my son play baseball, and generally squeeze every drop I can out of life."

It's not just cancer survivors who love Genentech. According to both *Science* and *Fortune* magazines, the company ranks as one of the best possible places to work. Employees are entitled to a list of perks that would make most American workers weep with envy: subsidized child care, $10,000 a year reimbursement for tuition, domestic partner benefits, free iced tea and espresso, fully paid gym memberships, discounted pet insurance, nursing mothers' rooms, etc.—not to mention generous health insurance and an annual three-week vacation. At Genentech, every day is casual Friday, and on Friday itself the company hosts a weekly social called a "Ho-Ho."

Then there's the food in the company cafeteria. Monday's offerings included "hazelnut beef stir-fry with sesame jasmine rice and soy beans" and "Caribbean spiced pork with apple-fennel chutney and sweet potato puree," for a mere $6, since Genentech picks up the rest of the tab. Or you might opt for the poached salmon or herb-crusted red snapper at $5 a shot, and dinner is served till 2 a.m.

But where there is food, there are food service workers, and the ones at Genentech don't experience the company as a life-giving force. It acts, in fact, as if it were determined to deny them any care. If this didn't show up in the *Science* and *Fortune* surveys of employee satisfaction, that's because Genentech's food service workers are subcontracted through a company called Guckenheimer Enterprises. Still, they're the ones who dish out the apple-fennel chutney in the cafeteria, and if they were to write a letter to Genentech for publication in the *New York Times*, it would go something like this statement from Milarose Oriel, age fifty-three (posted in full at www.theguckstopshere.info/pages/healthy.htm). "Dear Genentech," it would say:

I like working at the Genentech cafe, but our managers don't care about our health.

I had a stroke in 2001. This year, I asked for time off to see my doctor to get my blood pressure medicine refilled. But it's like Guckenheimer doesn't want me to see a doctor. First, my manager kept telling me to postpone my appointment, then I had to beg her to give me some time off. My doctor actually *called me* because he was worried. . . .

I got burned one morning in late January. Immediately, I reported the burn to the manager. I asked her to fill out an accident report, but she didn't. She gave me ointment and told me to go back to work. The next day I woke up with a fever and the burn was very painful. I asked her again to report it and she still said no.

When I met Milarose Oriel in San Francisco she told me she can't afford the insurance Guckenheimer offers, so she relies on temporary insurance provided by the county. In the last few weeks, since Oriel got interested in unionizing her coworkers, she's faced harassment at work—insults, nasty surprises, sudden loud noises—almost as if the company were trying to provoke another stroke.

Genentech claims to be neutral on the food service workers' organizing drive. It shrugs off the treatment of its food service workers, who are, after all, really the employees of Guckenheimer. But that excuse doesn't wash anymore. Whether it's the Gap or the University of Virginia, indignant citizens are demanding that companies take responsibility for their subcontracted labor. The scientists who work at Genentech need to know: there's blood in that chutney. Just as Genentech enabled Joel Golub to live to see his children's recitals and games, it needs to make sure that Milarose Oriel achieves her own dream: "to live to see her granddaughter grow up."

Workplace Bullies

IF THERE'S ONE THING WE KNOW ABOUT WORKPLACE bullying, it's that it tends to be inflicted by higher-ups on lower-downs. Executives might complain humorously of being bullied by their secretaries or even their housekeepers, but in real life bullying, like water, flows downhill. Busboys don't bully maitre d's.

This was my own experience of workplace bullying. When I took a low-wage waitressing job for *Nickel and Dimed*, my supervisor, a fortyish woman I'll call "B.J.," miffed by a perceived infraction—a chatty exchange with a fellow worker—rode me for an entire shift. First she upbraided me for an insufficient stack of napkins in the takeout area. Then, when I replenished them, she told me the stack was too high, and so forth on into the evening, while my fellow waitresses were rolling their eyes in mute solidarity. Just as I was getting ready to leave at the end of the shift, shaky-legged and punch-drunk from exhaustion, she announced that I needed to roll fifty more sets of silverware

and make up a fresh four-gallon batch of blue cheese dress-
ing. At an age when you're entitled to join the AARP, it's
humiliating to be kept after school.

There's a word for this sort of thing that goes beyond
bullying, with its implications of individual "bad apple"
behavior. The word is *rankism*, and it was coined by Robert
Fuller, the genial white-haired author of *Somebodies and
Nobodies: Overcoming the Abuse of Rank*. He's been a "some-
body"—president of Oberlin College—as well as a "nobody,"
and the transition between these statuses cued him into the
pervasiveness of rank in our supposedly democratic society.
It's not just race, sex, and class that determine your position—
but also where you stand in the organizational hierarchy.
Workplace bullying, he told me, is "archetypical rankism.
Hierarchy lends itself to abuse, and there are always people
who will take advantage."

But when I think of it, much more calmly now, I doubt
that B.J. could have been convinced that she was either bullying or taking advantage of the restaurant hierarchy. From
her point of view, she was just doing her job as a manager,
which was to extract as much labor from us as she could. I
hadn't been slacking off; my pal and I had been mopping
and lifting as we spoke. But even speaking—among low-
level employees—is often a no-no; in two places I worked
(though not this one) it was explicitly forbidden. If B.J. was
doing the right thing from a management perspective, then
we're faced with the question: Where do we draw the line
between bullying and official workplace policy?

Here's a kinky case from the blurred borderline between
bullying and business as usual. In 2006, fifty-four-year-old
Janet Orlando sued Alarm One, a California-based home
security company, for subjecting her to what could be
called motivational spankings. The spankings, usually

administered with the metal yard signs of competing companies, were part of a competition the company had set up between teams of salespersons, both men and women. As one salesman testified, "Basically, you'd get up in front of the room, put your hands on the wall, bend over, and get hit with the sign." Other punishments for underperforming salespersons included having eggs broken on their heads, having whipped cream sprayed on their faces, and being forced to wear diapers.

No individual was at fault here. It was company policy to spank people.

I could go on with examples of what could be called "bullyless bullying," in which no aberrant individual can be blamed. There's the matter of bathroom breaks, for example, which can be perilously infrequent, and not only for the elderly and the pregnant. The title of the one academic book on the issue tells it all: *Void Where Prohibited: Rest Breaks and the Right to Urinate on Company Time.* The authors, Marc Linder and Ingrid Nygaard, report that there are situations where women workers who are required to stand in one place for hours—cashiers and assembly line workers, for example—have taken to wearing adult diapers to work. At Alarm One, diapers were a punishment; for some employees, they're an everyday necessity, and there's not a "bully" in sight.

Workplace hierarchy doesn't have to be abusive. We've all had nurturing bosses as well as foul fiends. You can even make a good argument for a tight chain of command: it leads to speedier decisions and centralizes accountability. You wouldn't, for example, want your operation interrupted by lengthy democratic deliberations among the surgeons, technicians, and nurses. But—whether for reasons of profit, efficiency, or habit—higher-ups often treat lower-ranking folks disrespectfully or even abusively. Hierarchy nurtures the conditions for bullying.

We may be carrying hierarchy—and its evil twin, "rankism"—to an unnecessary extreme in the workplace. In a recent article, Howard Stein, an anthropologist at the University of Oklahoma, accuses American employers of creating a workplace culture of "organizational totalitarianism" marked by "degradation, intimidation, and terror," with the terror stemming from the constant threat of being fired, laid off, or "right-sized" out of a job. The result, he argues, is that, "in some sense, the spirits of tens of millions of American workers have been broken."

Employers take note: one of the first casualties of an overly authoritarian workplace is creativity and its byproduct, innovation. You're not going to venture a breakthrough idea if you know you'll be ignored or you won't get the credit for it or, for that matter, if your bladder is bursting. Which is why the most dynamic enterprises of recent years have been the dot-coms and other hi-tech companies, where dress codes and punch-in times are often abandoned for a freewheeling, less hierarchical corporate culture.

Authoritarian workplaces can also be counterproductive when the fine points of hierarchy—that is, office "politics"—begin to take precedence over getting the job done. In *The Office*, far more time goes into scheming and preening than into sales. Dilbert lives in a world dominated by clueless managers, where the underlings retreat into passive aggressiveness.

We might all be better off, current bullies included, in a culture that discouraged such pointless rankism. Robert Fuller thinks so and has launched a crusade he calls the "dignitarian movement," aiming for the recognition of each person's intrinsic value and contribution. It sounds a bit utopian, but as he points out, "We've made great progress against racism and sexism in recent decades. Now the time has come to do the same with rankism."

In some ways this may require heavier lifting than racism or sexism, since the victims don't form a visible constituency and are often deeply shamed by their status. But we can't put the job off much longer—there's far too much human dignity at stake.

Big (Box) Brother

I T READS LIKE A COLD WAR THRILLER: THE SPY FOLLOWS the suspects through several countries, ending up in Guatemala City, where he takes a room across the hall from his quarry. Finally, after four days of surveillance, including some patient ear-to-the-keyhole work, he is able to report back to headquarters that he has the goods on them. They're guilty!

But this isn't a John le Carré novel, and the powerful institution pulling the strings wasn't the USSR or the CIA. It was Wal-Mart, and the two suspects weren't carrying plans for a shoulder-launched H-bomb. Their crime was "fraternization." One of them, James W. Lynn, a Wal-Mart factory inspection manager, was traveling with a female subordinate, with whom he allegedly enjoyed some intimate moments behind closed doors. At least the company spy reported hearing "moans and sighs" within the woman's room.

Now you may wonder why a company so famously cheap that it requires its same-sex teams to share hotel rooms while on the road would invest in international espionage to ferret out mixed-sex fraternizers. Unless, as Lynn argues, they were really after him for what is a far worse crime in Wal-Mart's books: openly criticizing the conditions he found in Central American factories supplying Wal-Mart stores.

In fact, the cold war thriller analogy is not entirely fanciful. *New York Times* reporter Michael Barbaro, who related the story of Wal-Mart's stalking of Lynn and his colleague, also reports that the company's security department is staffed by former top officials of the CIA and the FBI. Along the same lines, the *New Yorker*'s Jeffrey Goldberg provides a chilling account of his visit to Wal-Mart's Bentonville "war room." Although instructed not to write down anything he saw, he found a "dark, threadbare room, . . . its walls painted battleship gray," where only two out of five of the occupants would even meet his eyes. In general, he found the Bentonville fortress "not unlike the headquarters of the National Security Agency."

We've always known that Wal-Mart is as big, in financial terms, as many sizable nations. It may even have begun to believe that it *is* one, complete with its own laws, security agency, and espionage system. But the illusion of state power is not confined to Wal-Mart. Justin Kenward, who worked at a Target store in Chino, California, for three years, wrote to tell me about his six-hour interrogation, in 2003, by the store's "asset protection" agents, who accused him of wrongly giving a fellow employee a discount on a video game a year earlier:

> After about an hour of trying to tell them that I don't remember anything about that day, let alone that transaction, I had to use the restroom. I asked if I could and was

denied. This goes on for about another hour when I say, "Look, I have to pee, bad, can I go to the restroom?" Once more I was told no. So I stand up and start walking out the door, and was stopped. At this point I thought to myself, "They're looking to fire me!" So I start to think of ways that transaction might have come to be. I say something like, "I would never give a discount unless an L.O.D. (Leader On Duty, aka a manager) or a Team Leader (aka supervisor) told me to." . . . I was interrupted and told that it sounds like I was trying to place my mistake on other people. Three hours into this and still needing to pee I was told that I need to write an apologetic letter to the company with the details, every detail, that we just went over. Then I could use the rest room.

Kenward lost his job.

My efforts to get a comment from Target were unavailing, but I did manage to track down a person who worked in security for the Chino store at the time of Kenward's detention. Because she still depends on Target for her health insurance, she asked not to be named, but she writes that Kenward's experience was not unusual. In one instance, she said, company security agents

took each of the twelve youngsters [Target employees who were suspected of stealing] to their office separately. They locked them in an office without a telephone, would not let them phone their parents or anyone, and kept them there browbeating them for six to ten hours. They never told them they were being arrested . . . only that Target was disappointed in them and if they would write a letter of apology that they'd dictate they could go and all would be forgotten. None of these children knew their rights . . . all of them ended up writing the stupid letter. Of course this too was a lie. . . . As soon as they had the letter in hand, the police were called and that person [who had written that particular letter] was hauled off in handcuffs and arrested.

This is the workplace dictatorship at its brass-knuckled best. When companies start imagining that they are nation-states, entitled to spy on, stalk, and interrogate their own employees, then we are well down the road to an actual, full-scale dictatorship.

As for those "moans and sighs" that issued from the hotel room in Guatemala City, maybe Lynn and his companion were reflecting on the sweatshop conditions they encountered in a Wal-Mart subcontractor's factory. Or maybe they were aware of the man spying on them and were mourning the decline of democracy.

Invasion of the Cheerleaders

D URING MY JOB SEARCH FOR *BAIT AND SWITCH*, I briefly considered applying for a position as a drug company sales rep. Why not? I have a BA in chemistry, which was listed on my résumé, and also—although unlisted—a PhD in biology. I love looking at chemical formulas and learning how a drug, for example, binds to a cell wall or an enzyme's active site. So I figured I'd be a crackerjack sales rep, capable of explaining to physicians how the addition of a methyl group to an existing drug molecule would make patients happier, more continent, virile, drynosed, or whatever the company promises.

There was just one problem: I am not now and have never been a cheerleader.

That's right, a cheerleader. The *New York Times* reports that drug companies are increasingly hiring college cheerleaders as their sales reps—to the point where there is a "recruiting pipeline" from college cheerleading squads direct to Big Pharma's sales force. One attraction of cheerleaders is simply that they're attractive, and doctors are still about 75 percent male.

But it's not just pretty faces and toned bodies that make cheerleaders good pharmaceutical sales reps. According to T. Lynn Williamson, a "cheering advisor" at the University of Kentucky, the drug company recruiters who approach him don't even ask what the cheerleader's college major was—chemistry, kinesthetics, hospitality management, it doesn't matter. "Proven cheerleading skills suffice," the *Times* comments, and in Williamson's words, these include "exaggerated motions, exaggerated smiles, exaggerated enthusiasm."

Cheerleaders, in other words, are the perfect exemplars of the ubiquitous advice to be perpetually cheerful and upbeat—at least if you want to get a job or hold on to one. Every career coach or motivational speaker will tell you that if you want to get ahead you need to act less like a chemist or IT person and more like a cheerleader.

All right, you can't sulk your way through a job interview or wear out your coworkers by moping eight hours a day. We all know that. But the corporations are asking much more from people now; they're demanding that we all become *actors*. If you don't feel wildly enthusiastic about marketing widgets or brokering life insurance, then you damn well better fake it.

This "theatricalization" of business raises all kinds of problems. Will that potentially hazardous, $300-a-month prescription drug actually help you, or was your doctor just charmed by a cheerleader's dazzling, gloss-enhanced smile? Are the tires on your car safe, or was someone at the auto company seduced by some Sarah Bernhardt of tire sales?

And then there are the psychological consequences of

acting as a way of life. For her classic 1983 study *The Managed Heart: Commercialization of Human Feeling,* sociologist Arlie Hochschild interviewed people who are required by their employers to exude emotions they may not feel—flight attendants, for example. (This was in the old days, before all the pay-cuts and pension thefts wiped the smiles off flight attendants' faces.) She concluded that constant emoting produces a kind of "emotional numbness," a reduced awareness of one's own feelings.

As for the effect on the "audience"—that is, those of us who are subjected to a steady display of "exaggerated smiles" and "exaggerated enthusiasm"—we get a little numb too. It doesn't take long to learn that a smile doesn't mean friendship, that wide-open eyes and exclamations of "awesome!" don't indicate the slightest interest. The entire emotional currency of human interaction is being fatally devalued, and when that happens there can be no trust. And when there is no trust there can be no business, no economy, no society worth living in.

But maybe I'm just an old sourpuss. Maybe the cheerleaders should take over the entire corporation. CEOs, for example, define much of their work as "motivational," which suggests it could be done just as well, if not better, by a peppy airhead in a microskirt. Nor should chemists be exempt from replacement by qualified cheerleaders. Give me a C! Give me an O! Give me an H!—and what have you got? If the ratios of the atoms are right, you've got sugar—or whatever that thick sticky syrup is that's gumming up corporate America.

Fake Your Way to the Top!

F IRST, STARTING WAY BACK IN THE 1950S, YOU HAD TO be "positive" to get ahead in business, ready to see the glass as half full even when it was lying shattered on the floor. Then, somewhere in the first few years of the twenty-first century, the bar was raised. It wasn't good enough to feel "positive" about spending your day doing cold calls to potential customers in Dayton—you be had to be "passionate" about it. And now, apparently, even that isn't good enough—you have to develop a YES! attitude, as in throwing back your head, balling up your fists, and screaming YESSS!!!

The purveyor of this new over-the-top, fanlike enthusiasm is Jeffrey Gitomer, in his *Little Gold Book of YES! Attitude*. What attracted me to the display in the bookstore was the odd packaging: a hardcover but smaller than the average paperback, with a bright red ribbon for a page marker (a biblical touch, someone in the publishing industry explained to me). Most of the pages contain less than two hundred words, but don't try filling in the margins with notes: the pages are too slick and shiny for your average pen, so if you want to make notes, get your own notebook.

How do you achieve a state of transcendent YES! excitement about your job? Brainwashing is recommended. Gitomer himself read Napoleon Hill's 1937 classic of delusional thinking, *Think and Grow Rich*, over a hundred times in one year and watched the same motivational video five days a week plus weekends. While reading the gurus and reciting the prescribed self-affirmations, it helps to cut off contact with the outer world. In particular, Gitomer says, don't watch the news. It's all "negative" anyway.

Of course you'll have to purge your environment of "negative" people too, as all the motivational gurus advise. Gitomer tells us he walks away from their "pity parties" to "focus on me." "Let nothing or no one get in your way."

Now, with Darfur, global warming, Iraq, and any recently bereaved or otherwise afflicted coworkers out of the way, you can "SMILE ALL THE TIME." "*A simple smile,*" Gitomer tells us, "*is a powerful atti-tool.*" Smiles "show your internal feelings, externally." And if you don't actually feel smiley internally, just fake it till you make it.

Nobody said it would be easy. In fact, the YES! attitude takes constant maintenance, and one of the illustrations shows Gitomer wearing a blue work shirt with the label "Positive Attitude Maintenance Department" on his chest. Read something "positive" every day, say "positive things all day long." Practice being "selfish *on the inside*" while exuding helpfulness on the outside.

Don't be distracted by this crude embrace of selfishness. What Gitomer and countless other motivational gurus are recommending is the mentality of a crafty slave: "Oh master, I am SO glad you transferred me to the Dayton accounts (even though they've been inactive for eighteen months), and, while I'm at it, would you like me to polish your shoes with my necktie?" Smiles, at least in human society, are gestures of submission and routinely demanded of women as a token of subordinate status. The happy slave smiles; the well-trained "lady" smiles; now even the male white-collar striver has to keep his lips pulled back in an expression of eager compliance. Only the top guys get to snarl and snap their way through the day.

But here's another idea, one that's every bit as "positive" as the gurus advise. Call it constructive complaining. Don't avoid "negative" people—seek them out and talk about what needs to be changed. Remember the movie *Nine to Five*, where the much put-upon characters played by Jane Fonda, Lily Tomlin, and Dolly Parton finally get together to share their woes and plan the overthrow of an abusive boss? Take your grievances seriously and turn that "pity party" into a revolutionary strategy meeting.

Challenging the Workplace Dictatorship

W HEN THE EMPLOYEE FREE CHOICE ACT CAME UP FOR consideration in the Senate, conservative columnist George F. Will suddenly developed a tender concern for workers' rights. The act, which would require employers to recognize a union whenever a majority of workers sign union cards–thus bypassing the often prolonged and creaky process of a National Labor Relations Board–supervised secret ballot vote–has stalled, in part because of critics like Will, who complained that it "strips all workers of privacy" and will repeal "a right to secret ballots–long considered fundamental to a democratic culture." As he put it, the unions are backing the act out of sheer desperation: since they can't seem to win a fair fight for workers' allegiance, they want government to take away the workers' rights and help herd them into union membership.

OK, now let's leave Will-land and enter an actual American workplace. Are you punched in? Good. The first thing to notice is that you've checked your basic civil rights at the

door. Freedom of speech? Forget about it: some employers
bar speech of any kind with your fellow employees. I saw
this firsthand at a chain restaurant and a big-box store.
Wanna work? Zip your lips.

How about those privacy rights that Will is so concerned
about? Nada—they don't exist outside of Will-land either.
You probably had to pee in a cup to get your job in the first
place, which constitutes a very intimate chemical invasion
of privacy. In most states, your purse or backpack can be
searched by the employer at any time; your e-mails and
Web activity can be monitored.

Right of assembly? Sorry, you don't have that either. In
my experience, most managers see a group of three or more
employees talking together as an insurrection in the making. Shut up and get back to work!

Since Will doesn't seem to know what happens before an
NLRB-supervised secret ballot vote, here's how it works.
During the increasingly prolonged lag between the initial
card signing and the actual vote, management uses every
means possible to intimidate, isolate, and harass the union's
supporters. Most commonly, workers are called away from
their jobs and required to attend management-run meetings where they are subjected to antiunion harangues and
videos. Note: not only do workers lack freedom of assembly, they lack the freedom to *not* assemble. If management
announces a 2 p.m. meeting, you better be there. These are
called "captive audience meetings" for a reason.

At the meetings, which may take place daily in the weeks
leading up to an NLRB election, management lays out a
dire picture of what will happen if the union comes in:
workers will lose the right to talk to managers individually
(not true); they will see their wages and benefits decline
(emphatically not true); they will be stuck paying exorbitant

dues (hardly); the company may have to move to Mexico. Sorry, no questions or comments from the audience.

Most prounion workers can withstand the company's mass-captive meetings. Harder to resist are the one-on-one and small group get-togethers, where individual workers are grilled about their union allegiance for as many hours as it takes. During one union drive among truck drivers, management confronted workers individually about personal issues like their credit ratings and family responsibilities. A lot of them finally broke down, and the union drive was defeated.

There's nothing wrong with management voicing its view on unions—say, in a flyer to workers—and certainly nothing wrong with secret ballots. The problem lies in the abuse of management power in the period leading up to the NLRB-sponsored vote, which can be months or years after the initial card signing. If workers are willing to sign a union card—which is a courageous step all by itself—that should be enough to signify their choice.

Will calls the Employee Free Choice Act "Orwellian." But Orwell's fascist *1984* is already here and it's called the American workplace. What really scares employers about the Employee Free Choice Act is that it will begin to reverse that—and bring the first stirrings of democracy to work.

Gap Kids: New Frontiers
in Child Abuse

IT WAS ENOUGH TO MAKE YOU VOMIT ALL OVER YOUR new denim jacket. The Gap has been caught using child labor in an Indian sweatshop, and not just child labor–child slaves. As extensively reported on the news, the children, some as young as ten, were worked sixteen-hour days, fed bowls of mosquito-covered rice, and forced to sleep on a roof and use overflowing latrines. Those who slowed down were beaten with rubber pipes and the ones who cried had oily cloths stuffed in their mouths.

But let's try to look at this dispassionately–not as a human rights issue but as a PR disaster, ranking right up there with the 1982 discovery of cyanide in Tylenol capsules. Think of this as a case study in a corporate Crisis Communication course: how is the Gap handling the problem, and could it do better?

This is not the first time the Gap has been caught using child labor, but Gap North America president Martha Hansen went on the air to state that the situation was "completely unacceptable" and that the company would "act swiftly." Her mistake was to get defensive about child labor, just as Kathie Lee Gifford did a few years ago when accused of using child labor in Honduras to manufacture her Kathie Lee line of clothing. Gifford broke into tears on TV, provoking malicious glee in her detractors. But the time has come to launch a full-throated defense of child labor.

If we could only get over our hypothetical qualms, the support for child labor would be enormous. After all, more and more American children are tried and punished as adults today. A ten-year-old Florida girl was arrested for carrying a steak knife in her lunch box; children have been Tasered. And the ubiquitous conservative pundit William Kristol will surely be enthusiastic, considering his recent—though possibly facetious—statement that, "whenever I hear anything described as a heartless assault on our children, I tend to think it's a good idea."

The core of the argument, though, is that anyone who opposes child labor has not witnessed its opposite, which is child unemployment and idleness. Think of it: 99 percent of child criminals are unemployed, as are 99 percent of obese children and schoolyard bullies. The remaining 1 percent are child actors, meaning they spend their time simulating unemployed children.

Hansen is a mother herself, but I wonder how often she has returned home from a hard day in the C-suites to find her unemployed offspring Magic Markering the walls and crushing the Froot Loops into the carpet. This is what jobless children do: they rub Krazy Glue into their siblings' hair; they spill apple juice onto your keyboard. Believe me, I see this kind of wantonly destructive behavior every day. Vandalism is a way of life for unemployed children, and they do not know the meaning of remorse.

In fact, corporate America should go further and make a strong statement against the sickening culture of dependency that has grown up around childhood. Why are jobless children so criminally inclined? Because they know that whatever damage they inflict, the Froot Loops will just keep coming. The Gap should portray its child-staffed factories as part of a far-seeing welfare-to-work program that will eventually be extended to American children as well.

To appeal to American parents, our own child factories should be run more like Montessori schools, where the children are already encouraged to regard every one of their demented activities as "work." If they're going to pile up blocks and knock them down all day, then why not sew on buttons and bring home a little cash? But even American families will have to brace themselves for the inevitable cost-cutting measures. First the cookies and milk may have to go, then, as in India, the toilets and beds. Wal-Mart has already pioneered the price-cutting defense of human rights abuses, and the Gap should follow suit.

The company can of course expect some lingering opposition. Just as there are vegetarians and pacifists, there will always be some men, for example, who would rather wear skirts than blue jeans impregnated with the excrement and tears of ten-year-olds. Well, let them shop at American Apparel or some other "sweat-free" vendor, and if they can't find anything there, let them wear dhotis. In a nation that cannot bring itself to extend child health insurance to all children in need, child-made clothes make a fine fashion statement.

French Workers Refuse
to Be "Kleenex"

W AS IT ONLY A FEW YEARS AGO THAT SOME OF OUR puffed-up patriots were denouncing the French as "cheese-eating surrender monkeys," too fattened on Camembert to stub out their Gauloises and get down with the war on Iraq? Well, take another look at the folks who invented the word *liberté*. When their government tried to strip them of the right to not be fired at an employer's whim—something Americans can only dream of—they marched, rioted, and burned up cars.

The French government's rationale for the new labor law that triggered the protests was economically impeccable, as economic reasoning goes these days: make it easier for employers to fire people and they will be more eager to hire people, thus reducing France's appalling unemployment rate of 9.6 percent. Furthermore, the law will apply only to people under twenty-six, and the terminations can occur only during the first two years of employment. So why was Paris burning?

Maybe the rioters sensed a logical fallacy in the government's proposal: fire more people so more people can be hired? What corporations call "flexibility"—the right to dispose of workers at will—is what workers experience as disposability, not to mention insecurity and poverty. The French students who tossed Molotov cocktails didn't want to become what they called "a Kleenex generation"—used and tossed away when the employer decides he needs a fresh one.

You may recognize in the French government's reasoning the same arguments Americans hear whenever we raise a timid plea for a higher minimum wage or a halt to the steady erosion of pensions and health benefits. What? scream the economists who flack for the employing class—if you do anything, anything at all, to offend or discomfit the employers they will respond by churlishly failing to employ you! Unemployment will rise, and you—lacking of course the health care and other benefits provided by the French welfare state—will quickly spiral down into starvation.

French youth didn't buy this kind of argument, probably because they knew where the "Anglo-Saxon model," as they call it, leads. If you have to give up job security to get a job, what next? Will the pampered employers be inspired to demand a suspension of health and safety regulations? Will they start requiring their workers to polish their shoes while hand-feeding them hot-buttered croissants? *Non* to all that, the French kids said. We only have to look to America—or, for that matter, China—to see where that will take us.

Of course the French weren't entirely fair in calling their nemesis the Anglo-Saxon model. It's the specifically American model they have to fear. I was giving a talk in England, ancestral home of the Anglo-Saxon race, when a fellow in the audience asked me how people could be fired without "due process." For a moment I thought I had misheard or been misled by one of those incomprehensibly quaint

English regional dialects. But no, in the UK a person who feels she has been wrongfully dismissed can turn to an employment appeals tribunal and, beyond that, to the courts. I had to explain that in the United States you can be fired for just about anything: having a "bad attitude," which can mean having a funny look on your face, or just turning out to be "not a good fit."

Years ago, there was a theory on the American left that someone—maybe it was me—termed worsism: the worse things get, the more likely people will be to rise up and demand their rights. But in America, at least, it doesn't seem to work that way. The worse things get, the harder it becomes even to imagine any kind of resistance. The fact that you can be fired "at will"—the will of the employer, that is—freezes employees into terrified obedience. Add to that the fact that job loss is accompanied by a loss of access to health care, and you get a kind of captive mentality bordering on the kinkily masochistic. Beat me, insult me, double my workload, but please don't set me free!

Far be it from me to advocate the burning of cars and smashing of store windows. But why did American students suck their thumbs when the Bush administration proposed a $12.7 billion cut in student loans? Where was the outrage over the massive layoffs at Ford, Hewlett-Packard, and dozens of other major companies? And was the poverty-stricken quarter of the population too stressed by their mounting bills and multiple jobs to protest cuts in Medicaid and already pathetic housing subsidies?

Compared to those "surrender monkeys," we're looking like a lot of soggy used Kleenex.

Truckers Protest,
the Resistance Begins

FOR TOO LONG, AMERICANS SEEMED TO HAVE NOTHING to say about their ongoing economic ruin except: Hit me! Please, hit me again! You can take my house, but let me mow the lawn for you one more time before you repossess. Take my job and I'll just slink off somewhere out of sight. Oh, and take my health insurance, too; I never could understand the deductible.

Then, in a wave of defiance, truck drivers began taking the strongest form of action they can take—inaction. Faced with diesel fuel prices at $4 per gallon, they slowed down, shut down, and started honking. On the New Jersey Turnpike, a convoy of trucks stretching "as far as the eye can see," according to a turnpike spokesman, drove at a glacial twenty miles an hour. Outside of Chicago, they slowed and drove three abreast, blocking traffic and taking arrests. They jammed into Harrisburg, Pennsylvania; they slowed down the Port of Tampa where fifty rigs sat idle in protest.

Near Buffalo, one driver told the press he was taking the week off "to pray for the economy."

The truckers who organized the protests—by CB radio and Internet—had a specific goal: reducing the price of diesel fuel. They are owner-operators, meaning they are also businesspeople, and with the high fuel costs, they couldn't break even. They wanted the government to release its fuel reserves. They wanted an investigation into oil company profits and government subsidies of the oil companies. Of the drivers I talked to, all were acutely aware that the government had found, in the course of a weekend, $30 billion to bail out Bear Stearns, while their own businesses were in a tailspin.

But the truckers' protests have ramifications far beyond the owner-operators' plight—first, because trucking is hardly a marginal business. You may imagine, in this Internet age, that everything important travels at the speed of pixels bouncing off satellites, but 70 percent of the nation's goods—from Cheerios to ChapStick—travel by truck. We were able to survive the writers' strike, but a truckers' strike would affect a lot more than your viewing options. As Donald Hayden, a Maine trucker, put it to me: "If all the truckers decide to shut this country down, there's going to be nothing they can do about it."

More important, the activist truckers understood their protest to be part of a larger effort to "take back America." One told me, "We continue to maintain this is not just about us." J.B.—which is his CB handle and stands for the "Jake Brake" on large rigs—said, "It's about everybody—the homeowners, the construction workers, the elderly people who can't afford their heating bills. . . . This is not the action of the truck drivers, but of the people." Hayden mentioned his parents, ages eighty-one and seventy-six, who had to get through the Maine winter on a fixed income. Missouri-based driver Dan Little talked about stores shutting down in his little town of Carrollton. "We're Americans," he said. "We built this country, and I'll be damned if I'm going to lie down and take this."

At least one of the truckers' tactics may be translatable to the foreclosure crisis. Hayden took the radical step of surrendering three rigs to be repossessed by Chrysler—only he did it publicly, with flair, right in front of the statehouse in Augusta. "Repossession is something people don't usually see," he said, and he wanted the state legislature to take notice. As he took the keys, the representative of Chrysler said, according to Hayden, "I don't see why you couldn't make the payments," to which Hayden responded, "See, I have to pay for fuel and food, and I've eaten too many meals in my life to give *that* up."

Suppose homeowners were to start making their foreclosures public events—inviting the neighbors and the press, at least getting someone to videotape the children sitting disconsolately on the steps and the furniture spread out on the lawn. Maybe, for a nice dramatic touch, having the neighbors shower the bankers, when they arrive, with dollar bills and loose change, since those bankers never can seem to get enough.

But the larger message of the truckers' protest is about pride or, more humbly put, self-respect, which these men have channeled from their roots. Dan Little told me, "My granddad said, and he was the smartest man I ever knew, 'If you don't stand up for yourself ain't nobody gonna stand up for you.'" Go to www.theamericandriver.com, run by J.B. and his brother in Texas, where you'll be greeted by a giant American flag, and you'll find—among the driving tips, weather info, and drivers' favorite photos—the entire

Constitution and Declaration of Independence. "The last time we faced something as impacting on us," J.B. said, "There was a revolution."

These actions were just the beginning. There was talk of a protest in Indiana, another in New York City, and a giant convergence of trucks on D.C. Who knows what it will all add up to? According to J.B., some of the big trucking companies were threatening to fire any of their employees who joined the owner-operators' protests.

But at least we've been given one shining example of defiance in the face of economic assault. There comes a point, sooner or later, when you stop scrambling around on all fours and, like J.B. and his fellow drivers all over the country, you finally stand up.

DECLINING
HEALTH

We Have Seen the Enemy—
and Surrendered

BOW YOUR HEADS AND RAISE THE WHITE FLAGS. AFTER
facing down the Third Reich, the Japanese empire, the
USSR, Manuel Noriega, and Saddam Hussein, the United
States has met an enemy it dares not confront: the American private health insurance industry.

The surrender buzz is everywhere. I heard it from a
notable liberal political scientist: we can't just leap to a
single payer system, he said in so many words, because it
would be too disruptive, given the size of the private health
insurance industry. Then I heard it from a Chicago woman
who leads a nonprofit agency serving the poor: how can we
go to a Canadian-style system when the private industry
has gotten so "big"?

Yes, it *is* big. Leighton Ku, at the Center for Budget and
Policy Priorities, gave me the figure of $776 billion in
expenditures on private health insurance for 2007. It's also
a big-time employer, paying about 400,000 people just to
turn down claims.

This in turn generates ever more employment in doctors' offices to battle the insurance companies. Dr. Atul Gawande, a practicing physician, wrote in the *New Yorker* that "a well-run office can get the insurer's rejection rate down from 30 percent to, say, 15 percent. That's how a doctor makes money. It's a war with insurance, every step of the way." And that's another thing your insurance premium has to pay for: the ongoing "war" between doctors and insurers.

Note: the private health insurance industry is not big because it relentlessly seeks out new customers. Unlike any other industry, this one grows by *rejecting* customers. No matter how shabby you look, Cartier, Lexus, or Nordstrom will happily take your money. Not Aetna. If you have a pre-existing condition, it doesn't want your business. Private health insurance is only for people who aren't likely ever to get sick. In fact, why call it "insurance," which normally embodies the notion of risk sharing? This is extortion.

Think of the damage. An estimated 18,000 Americans die every year because they can't afford, or can't qualify for, health insurance. That's the 9/11 carnage multiplied by six every year. Not to mention all the people who are stuck in jobs they hate because they don't dare lose their current insurance.

Saddam Hussein never killed 18,000 Americans or anything close; nor did the USSR. Yet we faced down those "enemies" with huge patriotic bluster, vast military expenditures, and, in the case of Saddam, armed intervention. So why does the United States soil its pants and cower in fear when confronted with the insurance industry?

Here's a plan. First, locate the biggest companies. No major intelligence effort will be required, since Google should suffice. Second, estimate their armed strength. No doubt there are legions of security guards involved in

protecting the company headquarters from irate consumers, but these should be manageable with a few
brigades. Next, consider an air strike, followed by an
infantry assault.

And what about those 400,000 people who are paid just
to say no to the rest of us? Well, I have a plan for them: it's
called *unemployment.* I'm not mean, though. If we had universal, single-payer health insurance, private health insurance workers would continue to be covered after they are
laid off. And I'd even recommend a job training program
for out-of-work health insurance company executives—
perhaps as home health aides.

Fellow citizens, where is the old macho spirit that has
sustained us through countless conflicts against enemies
both real and imagined? In the case of health care, we have
identified the enemy, and the time has come to crush it.

Gouging the Poor

THERE'S MORE AND MORE WHINING ABOUT HEALTH care: the shocking cost of insurance, the mounting reluctance of employers to share that cost, the challenge, should you be so lucky as to have insurance, of finding a doctor your insurance company will deign to reimburse, and so forth. But let's look at the glass half full for a change. Despite the growing misfit between health care costs and personal incomes, it is not yet illegal to be sick.

Not quite yet, anyway, though the trend is clear: hospitals are increasingly resorting to brass knuckle tactics to collect overdue bills from indigent patients. Take the case of an intermittently insured mechanic with diabetes who, as reported in the *Wall Street Journal,* ran up a $579 debt to Carle Hospital in Champaign-Urbana. When he failed to appear for a court hearing on his debt rather than miss a day of work, he was arrested and hit with $2,500 bail. Arrests for missed court dates, which the hospitals whimsically refer to as "body attachments," are on the rise throughout the country. Again, on the half-full side, we should be thankful that the bodies attached by hospitals cannot yet be used as sources of organs for transplants.

Mindful of their status as nonprofit, charitable institutions, hospitals used to be relatively congenial creditors. My uninsured companion of several years would simply work out a payment arrangement—on the scale of about $25 a month for life—and receive the necessary care without concern for his freedom. No longer, and it's not just the dodgier, second-rate hospitals that are relying on the police as collection agents. In the space of three years, Yale–New Haven Hospital, for example, obtained sixty-five arrest warrants for delinquent debtors. Of course, if you happen to work for a hospital, it's not your body that gets "attached." On a visit to Yale hospital workers, I met Tawana Marks, a registrar at the hospital who had the misfortune to also be admitted as a patient. Unsurprisingly, her hospital-supplied health insurance failed to cover her hospital-incurred bill, so Marks now has her paycheck garnished by her own employer—a condition of debt servitude reminiscent of early-twentieth-century company towns.

Furthermore, it turns out that, to compound the sufferings of the sick and subaffluent, hospitals now routinely charge uninsured people several times more than the insured. The *Fort Lauderdale Sun-Sentinel* reports that one local hospital charged an uninsured patient $29,000 for an appendectomy that would have cost an insured patient $6,783. According to the *Los Angeles Times*, in one, albeit for-profit, California hospital chain, the uninsured account for only 2 percent of its patients, but 35 percent of its profits.

The explanation for such shameless gouging of the poor? Big insurance companies and HMOs are able to negotiate "discounts" for their members, leaving the uninsured to pay whatever fanciful amounts the hospital cares to charge, such as, in one reported case, $50 for the use of a hospital gown.

Back in 1961, psychiatrist Thomas Szasz noted the "medicalization" of behavior formerly classified as crime or sin, such as drug addiction or what was then defined as sexual deviance. Rather than see this as a benign and potentially merciful trend, the crotchety Szasz complained about the growing concentration of power in the hands of a "therapeutic state." How quaint his concern sounds today, when instead of the medicalization of crime we are faced with the criminalization of illness.

Because almost everyone, no matter how initially healthy and prosperous, is now in danger of falling into the clutches of the medical/penitentiary system. It could start with a condition—say, high blood pressure or diabetes—serious enough to be entered into your medical record. Next you lose your job, and with it your health insurance, or—as in the case of a thousand or so freelance writers (including myself) once insured through the National Writers Union—the insurance company simply decides it no longer wants your business. You go to get new insurance but, wait, no one wants you because you now have a preexisting condition. So when that condition flares up or is joined by a new one, you enter the hospital as a "self-pay" patient, incur bills four times higher than an insured patient would, fall behind in paying them, and, given the hospitals' predatory collection tactics, wind up in jail.

Sociologists have long seen a connection between sickness and criminality, classifying both as forms of "deviance." Certainly the relevant vocabularies have been converging: note the similarity between the phrases *preexisting condition* and *prior conviction*, as well as the use of the terms *record* and *case*. A doctor once told me that, although he had detected a new and potentially life-threatening condition, he would refrain from prescribing anything to correct it, lest my record be marred by yet another preexisting condition.

The day will come when we look back on such small acts of kindness with nostalgia. Even as I write this, some bright young MBA at Aetna or Prudential is no doubt coming to the conclusion that a great deal of money and valuable medical resources could be saved through the simple expedient of arresting people at the first sign of illness. Skip the intermediate stages of diagnostic testing, hospitalization, and attempted debt collection and proceed directly to incarceration. The result will be the same, unless you succeed in concealing that cough or unsightly swelling from the cop on his or her beat.

I'm prepared for this eventuality, having been raised by a mother who was in turn raised by her Christian Scientist grandparents and had thus been trained to greet her children's symptoms with contempt and derision. I was conditioned, in other words, to conflate physical illness with moral failure. So should a rash or sore throat arrive, I stand ready, at some deep psychic level, to serve my time.

But for those of you who still imagine that illness and pain should elicit kindly responses from one's fellow humans, I have one last half-full observation: our prisons do offer health care—grossly inadequate care, to be sure, but at least it's free—even for child molesters, ax murderers, and those miscreants who have the gall to be both sick and uninsured.

The High Cost of Doing without Universal Health Care

Here's the news that just shook my little world: we got a message that a family friend, let's call her Lorraine, was in an ICU, barely able to breathe on her own. In the last few weeks, there'd been some mumblings about "not feeling a hundred percent," but no hint of anything seriously wrong. The diagnosis came back in a couple of days: fourth-stage breast cancer that had spread to a number of other organs, including her lungs. If you know anything at all about breast cancer "staging," you know there is no fifth stage.

Lorraine, it turns out, has no health insurance. We didn't know that—in fact, we'd been content to believe that her consulting business was going as well as she said it was. In her late forties now, she's a former accountant who never could find another decent job. She's also a news junkie, an avid reader, and an energetic volunteer in a number of worthy causes. She's usually balancing a half dozen projects at a time and is ebullient about all of them.

But it turns out she's been struggling with the cell phone bill and the rent. Unbeknownst to us, she'd recently moved out of her apartment and into a free room offered by one of the nonprofits she volunteers for. The cost of a mammogram—close to $300—must have been out of reach.

Any discussion of health plans needs to include Lorraine. One concept, favored by conservatives, is that we should each have a "catastrophic" health insurance policy for the big-ticket items like breast cancer, plus a tax-deductible savings account for the little things, like mammograms. If we have to take "personal responsibility" for our doctor visits and routine care we'll be thrifty about it—or so the thinking goes—and the nation's medical expenditures will stop spiking like an Ebola fever.

It's an old idea, going back at least to the Clintons, that the problem with the American health system is that we, the consumers, just consume too much. Make us mindful of the costs by raising copayments and other out-of-pocket costs, and we'll stop indulging in blood workups, MRIs, prostate exams, and all those other fun things.

But, as with Lorraine, when the price gets too high, there's no consumption at all. Lorraine's problem wasn't that she feasted on unnecessary care but that, like so many other of the 47 million uninsured Americans, she just wasn't getting any care. Maybe, when she first noticed the lump, she should have staged a sit-in at the nearest clinic until they sprang for a free mammogram. But her idea of "personal responsibility" was not to be a bother to anyone.

And how much does the "personal responsibility" theory even apply to the insured population? I have insurance, but that doesn't mean I determine what care I consume. It's not my idea to have an annual mammogram and Pap smear. The doctor had to threaten tears before I'd submit to a bone scan, and they'll have to drag me in for a colonoscopy. No one aside from the rare victim of Munchausen's syndrome goes looking for recreational medical care.

The fact is there's a big difference between the economics of health care and that of, say, costume jewelry. We the consumers control the demand for costume jewelry; we can splurge on it or leave it alone. But it's the medical profession that determines what health care we consume. Sure, we can take personal responsibility by exercising and refraining from smoking and skydiving or swimming with sharks. We can eat right, too (whatever that may mean, with the dietary advice fluctuating from month to month). But doctors have the last say on how often we need our blood drawn, our breasts squished, our cervices scraped, or any of the other unpleasant interventions they have to offer.

If the amount of medical care we consume were under our own control, I'd say, Sure, save up for it and use it wisely. But it's no more in our control than the wind and floods we insure our homes against. Accidents strike, along with mortal illnesses, and it's up to someone else to decide how much and what kind of treatments we'll need. When something is not in our control, we spread the risk with some form of insurance. We don't say, Save up because you're on your own.

You think universal health insurance is too expensive? Let's be hardheaded about Lorraine's case. If she'd been diagnosed earlier, she might have gotten by with a mastectomy and a bout of chemotherapy instead of burning up Medicaid dollars in an ICU. She might be out volunteering for the needy right now, instead of lying in terror in a hospital bed.

Health Care vs. the Profit Principle

I T'S ALWAYS NICE TO SEE A PRESIDENT TAKE A PRIN-cipled stand on something. The man formerly known as "43," and perhaps better remembered as "29" for his record–breaking approval rating, promised to battle any expansion of government health insurance for children–and not because he hates children or refuses to cough up the funds. No, this was a battle over principle: private health care vs. government-provided health care. Speaking to an audience in Cleveland, Bush boldly asserted:

I strongly object to the government providing incentives for people to leave private medicine, private health care to the public sector. And I think it's wrong and I think it's a mistake. And therefore, I will resist Congress's attempt . . . to federalize medicine. . . . In my judgment that would be–it would lead to not better medicine but worse medicine. It would lead to not more innovation but less innovation.

Now, as anyone who's ever had a dustup over their medical bills knows, if there is one area of human endeavor where private enterprise doesn't work, it's health care. Consider the private, profit-making insurance industry that Washington so strenuously defends. What "innovations" has it produced? The deductible, the copay, and the preexisting condition are the only ones that leap to mind. In general, the great accomplishment of the private health insurance industry has been to overturn the very meaning of "insurance": we all put in some money, though only some of us will need to draw on the common pool by using expensive health care. And the insurance companies have further overturned it by refusing to insure the people who need care the most—those who are already, or are likely to become, sick.

This is not because health insurance executives are meaner than other people, although I do not rule that out. It's just that they're running a business, the purpose of which is not to make people healthy but to make money, and they do very well at that. Once, many years ago, I complained to the left-wing economist Paul Sweezey that America had no real health system. "We have a system all right," he responded. "It's just a system for doing something else." A system, as he might have put it, for extracting money from the vulnerable and putting it into the pockets of the rich.

But let's not just pick on the insurance companies, though I wouldn't mind doing that—with a specially designed sharp instrument, over a period of years. The *Los Angeles Times* has reported a particularly lurid case of medical profiteering in the form of one Dr. Prem Reddy, who owns eight hospitals in Southern California. I do not begrudge any physician a comfortable lifestyle—good doctoring is hard work—but Dr. Reddy dwells in a 15,000-square-foot mansion featuring gold-plated toilets and keeps a second home, valued at more than $9 million, in Beverly Hills, as well as a $1.4 million helicopter for commuting.

The secret behind his $300 million fortune? For one thing, he rejects the standard hospital practice of making contracts with insurance companies, because he feels that these contracts unduly limit his reimbursements. (In a battle between Aetna and Reddy, it would be hard to know which side to cheer for.) In addition, he's suspended much-needed services such as chemotherapy, a birthing center, and mental health care as insufficiently profitable. And his hospitals are infamous for refusing to treat uninsured patients, like a patient with kidney failure and a sixteen-month-old baby with a burn.

But Dr. Reddy—who is, incidentally, a high-powered Republican donor—has a principled reason for his piratical practices. According to the *Los Angeles Times*, he believes that patients "may simply deserve only the amount of care they can afford." He dismisses as "an entitlement mentality" the idea that everyone should be getting the same high-quality health care. This is the vaunted conservative principle of "private medicine" at its nastiest: You don't get what you need, only what you can pay for.

If government insurance for children isn't expanded to all the families that need it, there is no question but that some children will die—painfully perhaps and certainly unnecessarily. But at least they will have died for a principle.

Children Deserve
Veterinary Care Too

In 2007, Americans spent about $10 billion on health care for their pets, up from $7.2 billion five years earlier. According to the *New York Times*, New York's leading pet hospitals offer CT scans, MRIs, dialysis units, and even a rehab clinic featuring an underwater treadmill, perhaps for the amphibians in one's household. A professor who acts as a consultant to pet health facilities justified these huge investments in pet health to me by pointing out that pets are, after all, "part of the family."

Well, there's another category of creatures that might reasonably be considered "part of the family." True, they are not the ideal companions for the busy young professional: it can take two to three years to housebreak them, their standards of personal hygiene are lamentably low, at least compared with cats, and large numbers of them cannot learn to "sit" without the aid of Ritalin.

I'm talking about children, of course, and while I can understand why many people would not want one of these hairless and often incontinent bipeds in their homes, it is important to point out that they can provide considerable gratification. There's a three-year-old in my life, for example, who gives me many hours a week of playful distraction from the pressures of work. No matter how stressed I am, she can brighten my mood with her quavering rendition of "Somewhere Over the Rainbow."

She has health insurance, as it turns out, and generally high-quality care. But you can never be too sure. So I went to the Web site of VPI Pet Insurance, one of the nation's largest animal companion health insurers, to see what kind of a policy I could get for her. In the application form, I listed her as a three-year-old mixed-breed dog—a description made somewhat plausible by the fact that her first words, spoken at the remarkable age of ten months, were "ruf ruf" and "doggie outside." When I completed the form and clicked to get a quote I was amazed to see that I could get her a "premium" policy for a mere $33 a month.

But, you may be wondering, can a veterinarian handle common childhoods ills? On the hopeful side, let me cite the case, reported by Bob Herbert of the *New York Times*, of Diamonte Driver, a twelve-year-old boy who died from an abscessed tooth because he had no insurance and his mother could not afford $80 to have the tooth pulled. Could a vet have handled this problem? Yes, absolutely.

Or there's the case of fourteen-year-old Devante Johnson, also reported by Herbert, who died when his health insurance ran out in the middle of treatment for kidney cancer. I don't know exactly what kind of treatment he was getting, but I suspect that the $1.25 million linear accelerator for radiation therapy available at one of New York's leading pet hospitals might have helped. The *Times* article on pet health also mentions a mixed breed named

Bullwinkle who consumed $7,000 worth of chemotherapy before passing on to his reward. Surely Devante could have benefited from the same kind of high-quality care, delivered at an upscale animal hospital.

It may seem callous to focus on children when so many pets go uninsured and without access to CT scans or underwater treadmills. But in many ways, children stack up well compared with common pets. They can shed real tears, like Vietnamese pot-bellied pigs. They can talk as well as many of the larger birds, or at least mimic human speech. And if you invest enough time in their care and feeding, they will jump all over you, yipping and covering your face with drool, when you arrive at the door.

In 2007, the Senate Finance Committee approved a bill that would expand state health insurance coverage for children to include 3.2 million kids who were not covered (but leaving about 6 million still uncovered). Then-president Bush vetoed the bill, on the grounds that government should not be involved in health coverage. Clearly, the time has come for a new demand. *Make pet health insurance available to all American children now!* Though even as I say this, I worry that some cost-conscious conservatives will counter by proposing to extend euthanasia services to children who happen to fall ill.

Our Broken Mental Health System

O N APRIL 16, 2007, A WITHDRAWN, SILENT KID NAMED Cho Seung-Hui opened fire on the Virginia Tech campus, killing thirty-two people. Leaving aside the issue of WMM (Weapons of Mass Murder, aka guns), the massacre has something to teach us about the American mental health system. It's farcically easy for an American to be diagnosed as mentally ill: all you have to do is squirm in your fourth grade seat and you're likely to be hit with the label of ADD and a prescription for an antipsychotic. But when a genuine whack job comes along–the kind of guy who calls himself "Question Mark" and turns in essays on bloodbaths–there's apparently nothing to be done.

While Cho Seung-Hui quietly–very quietly–pursued his studies, millions of ordinary, nonviolent folks were being subjected to heavy-duty labels ripped from the DSM-IV. An estimated 20 percent of American children and teenagers are diagnosed as mentally ill in the course of a year, and adults need not feel left out of the labeling spree:

watch enough commercials and you'll learn that you suffer from social phobia, depression, stress, or some form of sexual indifference (at least I find it hard to believe that all this "ED" is purely physical in origin).

Consider the essay "Manufacturing Depression" that appeared in *Harper's.* Hoping to qualify for a study on "Minor Depression" at the Massachusetts General Hospital, the author, Gary Greenberg, presented a list of his problems, including "the stalled writing projects and the weedy garden, the dwindling bank accounts and the difficulties of parenthood," in other words, "the typical plaint and worry and disappointment of a middle-aged, middle-class American life." Alas, it turned out he did not qualify for the Minor Depression study. "What you have," the doctor told him, "is Major Depression."

A number of psychiatrists have pointed out that the real business of the mental health system is social control. Normal, physically active nine-year-olds have to be taught to sit still. Adults facing "dwindling bank accounts" have to be drugged or disciplined into accepting their fate. What therapy aims to achieve is not "health" but compliance with social norms. The idea still rings true every time I've been confronted with a "personality test" that reads like a police interrogation: How much have you stolen from previous employers? Do you have any objections to selling cocaine? Is it "easier to work when you're a little bit high"?

Then there is the ubiquitous Myers-Briggs test, which seems obsessed with weeding out loners. Presumably, someone in the HR department can use your test results to determine whether you're a good "fit." (Incidentally, Myers-Briggs possesses no category for and no means of detecting the person who might show up at work one day with an automatic weapon.)

But for all the attention to "personality" and garden-variety neurosis, we are left with the problem of the afore-mentioned whack jobs, and the painful question remains: if Cho Seung-Hui's oddities had been noted earlier—say, when he was still under eighteen—could he have been successfully diagnosed and treated? Journalist Paul Raeburn's 2004 book, *Acquainted with the Night: A Parent's Quest to Understand Depression and Bipolar Disorder in His Children*, suggests that the answer is a resounding no.

When his own children started acting up, Raeburn found that there are scores of therapists listed in the Yellow Pages, as well as quite a few inpatient facilities for the flamboyantly symptomatic. But nothing linked these various elements of potential care into anything that could be called a "system." The therapists, who all march to their own theoretical and pharmaceutical drummers, have no reliable connections to the hospitals, nor do the hospitals have any means of providing follow-up care for patients after they are discharged.

Then there is the matter of payment. As managed care plans gained ground in the health care system in the 1990s, Raeburn reports, they cut their spending on psychiatric treatment by 55 percent, putting mental health services almost out of the reach of the middle class, never mind the poor. Hence, no doubt, the fact that three-quarters of children and teenagers who receive a diagnosis of mental illness get no care for it at all.

If we have no working mental health system, and no means of detecting or treating the murderously disturbed, then here's yet another argument for doing what we should do anyway: limit access to the tools of murder, end the casual sale of handguns.

What Causes Cancer: Probably Not You

THE PERENNIAL TEMPTATION TO BLAME DISEASE ON sin or at least some grave moral failing has recently taken another hit. A major new study shows that women on a virtuous low-fat diet with an extraordinary abundance of fruits and veggies were no less likely to die of breast cancer than women who grazed more freely. Media around the world have picked up on the finding, still cautioning, prudishly, that you can't beat breast cancer with cheeseburgers and beer either.

Another "null result" in cancer studies—that is, one showing that a suspected correlation isn't there—has received a lot less attention. In the May 2007 issue of *Psychological Bulletin,* James Coyne and his colleagues at the University of Pennsylvania reported that "there is no compelling evidence linking psychotherapy or support groups with survival among cancer patients." This finding flies in the face of the received wisdom that any sufficiently sunny-tempered person can beat cancer simply with a "positive attitude." For example, an e-zine article entitled "Breast Cancer Prevention Tips" advises:

> A simple positive and optimistic attitude has been shown to reduce the risk of cancer. This will sound amazing to many people; however, it will suffice to explain that several medical studies have demonstrated the link between a positive attitude and an improved immune system. Laughter and humor has been shown to enhance the body's immunity and prevents against cancer and other diseases. You must have heard the slogan "happy people don't fall sick."

So far no one appears to have read Coyne's study. A month after its publication, all-purpose guru Deepak Chopra assured Sanjay Gupta on CNN that the mind can control the body: "You know, of course, the . . . study where women who supported each other in a loving environment with breast cancer, the survival doubled." Gupta, last sighted seeking to discredit Michael Moore's *Sicko* with his "fact-checking," simply nodded, although the study Chopra was referring to was discredited years before Coyne's research came out.

For the last decade or so, adherents of the new discipline of "positive psychology" have been insisting that not just cancer but almost any other health setback can be conquered with optimism or a positive attitude. But as Coyne and other critics point out, the science here is shaky at best. Even the theoretical linchpin of the supposed happy-mind-healthy-body connection—that a positive outlook strengthens the immune system—took a kick in the teeth a few years ago when Suzanne Segerstrom at the University of Kentucky found, to her own apparent surprise, that optimism can have a negative effect on the immune system when the stressors are intense, as in the case of serious disease.

Even if veggies and smiles don't cure cancer, aren't we still entitled to blame some people for their diseases? Lack of exercise and dietary indiscretions play a role in the development of diabetes and coronary heart disease, so we indulge in self-gratifying contempt for the fat lady scarfing down Doritos. But before you rush to judgment, remember that nutritional alternatives are often unavailable and usually a lot more expensive. As for exercise, gym memberships easily cost $500 a year, and far too many of us are forced to spend ten hours or more a day sitting in a cubicle, a car, or a bus.

In the case of breast cancer, one victim-blaming theory after another has wilted under scrutiny. The "cancer personality" theory, for example, which breast cancer victim Susan Sontag took on in her 1978 book *Illness as Metaphor*, and now high-fat diets and negative attitudes. Something other than genetics causes it, though, and one leading candidate is the hormone replacement therapy that doctors pushed on menopausal women for decades as a supposed way of preventing heart disease, Alzheimer's, and wrinkles. When, in 2002, HRT was found to be correlated with breast cancer and millions of women stopped taking it, the incidence of breast cancer plunged.

Which suggests that optimism, especially about the validity of the conventional wisdom, can be hazardous. What you need is a narrow-eyed, deeply skeptical attitude.

Liposuction: The Key to Energy Independence

EVERYONE TALKS ABOUT OUR TERRIBLE DEPENDENCY on oil—foreign and otherwise—but hardly anyone mentions what it *is*. Fossil fuel, all right, but whose fossils? Mostly tiny plants called diatoms, but quite possibly a few Barney-like creatures went into the mix, like stegosaurus, brontosaurus, or other giant reptiles that shared the Jurassic period with all those diatoms. What we are burning in our cars and using to heat or cool our homes is, in other words, a highly processed version of corpse juice.

Think of this for a moment, if only out of respect for the dead: There you were, about a hundred million years ago, maybe a contented little diatom or a great big brontosaurus stumbling around the edge of a tar pit—a lord of the earth. And what are you now? A sludge of long-chain carbon molecules that will be burned so that some mammalian biped can make a CVS run for Mountain Dew and chips.

It's an old human habit, living off the roadkill of the planet. There's evidence, for example, that early humans were engaged in scavenging before they figured out how to hunt for themselves. They'd scan the sky for circling vultures, dash off to the kill site—hoping that the leopard that did the actual hunting had sauntered off for a nap—and gobble up what remained of the prey. It was risky, but it beat doing your own antelope tracking.

We continue our career as scavengers today, attracted not by vultures but by signs saying "Safeway" or "Giant." Inside these sites, we find bits of dead animals wrapped neatly in plastic. The killing has already been done for us—usually by underpaid immigrant workers rather than leopards.

I say to my fellow humans: It's time to stop feeding off the dead and grow up! I don't know about food, but I have a plan for achieving fuel self-sufficiency in less time than it takes to say "Arctic National Wildlife Refuge." The idea came to me from reports of the growing crime of french fry oil theft: Certain desperate individuals are stealing restaurants' discarded cooking oil, which can then be used to fuel cars. So the idea is: Why not skip the french fry phase and harvest high-energy hydrocarbons right from ourselves?

I'm talking about liposuction, of course, and it's a mystery to me why it hasn't occurred to any of those geniuses who are constantly opining about fuel prices on MSNBC. The average liposuction removes about half a gallon of liquid fat, which may not seem like much. But think of the vast reserves our nation is literally sitting on! Thirty percent of Americans are obese, or about ninety million individuals or forty-five million gallons of easily available fat—not from dead diatoms but from our very own bellies and butts.

This is the humane alternative to biofuels derived directly from erstwhile foodstuffs like corn. Biofuels, as you might have noticed, are exacerbating the global food crisis by turning edible plants into gasoline. But we could put humans back in the loop by first turning the corn into Fritos and hence into liposuctionable body fat. There would be a reason to live again, even a patriotic rationale for packing on the pounds.

True, liposuction is not risk free, as the numerous doctors' Web sites on the subject inform us. And those of us who insist on driving gas guzzlers may quickly deplete their personal fat reserves, much as heroin addicts run out of useable veins. But the gaunt, punctured look could become a fashion statement. Already, the combination of a tiny waist and a huge carbon footprint—generated by one's Hummer and private jet—is considered a sign of great wealth.

And think what it would do for our nation's self-esteem. We may not lead the world in scientific innovation, educational achievement, or low infant mortality, but we are the global champions of obesity. Go to http://www.nationmaster .com/graph/hea_obe-health-obesity and you'll find America well ahead of the pack when it comes to personal body fat, while those renowned oil-producers—Saudi Arabia, Venezuela, and Iran—aren't even among the top twenty-nine. All we need is a healthy dose of fat pride and for CVS to start marketing home liposuction kits. That run for Mountain Dew and chips could soon be an energy-neutral proposition.

A Society That Throws
the Sick Away

MOST COUNTRIES ARE PROUD TO HAVE A HEALTH care system. It's an organized way of helping the sick and infirm—a mark of genuine civilization. Not so here, alas, where the health system is rapidly becoming a health *hazard*. After decades of privatizing, profiteering, and insurance company–driven bureaucratization, Florence Nightingale has morphed into Vampira.

Health care costs are sucking the blood out of the economy, for one thing. Consider poor General Motors, once America's flagship corporation and now sinking under the weight of its employee health benefits—which account for at least $1,500 of the sticker price of each new vehicle. As GM proceeds with mass layoffs, other companies thrash around frantically trying to shed their insurance-needy American employees. They downsize and outsource—anything to escape the burden of health costs. Hence, in no small part, the "jobless recovery" of the early 2000s. Companies don't want to assume responsibility for their workers' medical bills and—this being the global temple of free enterprise—neither does the government.

Then there are the US health system's toxic effects on individuals, and I'm not referring to Vioxx or the approximately 200,000 people who die each year as a result of "medical mistakes." Harvard's Elizabeth Warren has shown that more than half of all bankruptcies are triggered by medical costs, and it's easy enough to see how. If you lose your job—through, say, downsizing or outsourcing—you lose your health insurance, and the uninsured routinely pay more than the insured. As for emergency rooms, which the hard-hearted or incurious imagine absorbing all the poor and uninsured—well, the average visit to an ER now costs a little over $1,000, which is a high price to pay for an asthma attack or an infant's fever.

Certainly the health system makes plenty of people rich—Big Pharma's overlords, for example, and insurance company CEOs—but it makes a lot more people poor—indirectly, by inhibiting job growth, and directly, by grinding individuals down to bankruptcy (which, thanks to the 2005 federal bankruptcy law, offers no fresh start to the debt-ridden). Add to this the well-known fact that poverty is a risk factor for dozens of diseases—from asthma to AIDS, from depression to diabetes—and, well, I rest my case.

When doctors notice a tissue growing nonstop—as US medical costs are doing—and in the process draining nutrients from the body as a whole, they insist on prompt excision, that is, cutting the thing out before it kills. So, too, one might think, economists should be calling for the immediate destruction of the American health care system. Stamp it out and drive a stake through its heart! Since Americans will still need health care, the solution is obvious: if we can't outsource our illnesses—and there is so far no technology for transferring one's cancer or atrial fibrillation to a starving African or Asian—we can at least outsource our health care.

It's already happening, in fact, though only in a helter-skelter way. An estimated two million Americans cross the borders annually to purchase their prescription meds in Mexico or Canada. US X-rays are increasingly interpreted by radiologists in India. Patients are being globalized, too, as hundreds of thousands of them from all parts of the world flock to Manila, Singapore, Bangalore, and other centers of low-cost, high-quality care. Some hospitals in India lure the rich with airport-to-hospital-bed car service and postsurgical yoga holidays, and I can foresee cheap, Motel 6–style hospitals springing up in Tijuana for the American working class.

All right, it's painful to admit that the nation that produced Jonas Salk, pacemakers, and MRIs can't do health care anymore. But there are other things we don't do here much anymore, like manufacturing. In the case of health care, it wasn't the science that foiled us (though, with more schools teaching only biblically approved versions of biology, that may soon be a problem too). No, we Americans just couldn't figure out the technology for distributing health care to the people who need it. We left the whole business to business, and business screwed it up.

The abolition of the American health care system will lead to some difficult readjustments, of course. Our doctors, nurses, and technicians, who are among the best trained in the world, will have to seek work in the emerging Asian centers of medical tourism. As for the insurance company functionaries whose sole business it is to turn down your claims, they may be bit harder to reemploy, since they have no counterpart in any civilized, health-providing nation.

GETTING SEX STRAIGHT

Fear of Restrooms

I DON'T SUFFER FROM FEAR OF FLYING—IT'S FEAR OF AIR-
ports that cripples me. Anything could happen to you in
an airport: you could be apprehended by the TSA, the
DEA, or, as we learned from the Larry Craig case, the vice
squad. I'm at the point where I'm beginning to develop subsidiary phobias—to Cinnabon, Sbarro, and, most recently,
airport restrooms.

I don't know whether lesbians hook up in airport ladies'
rooms. Judging from my lesbian friends, they don't do
much hooking up at all. They fall in love, move in together,
and start devoting themselves to home improvements and
weekends at Lowe's. But if they do, on occasion, cruise airport restrooms in the manner of a US senator, what signal-
ing techniques do they use? And could I have inadvertently
been employing them?

Because, face it, how many of us knew that the way to
attract a fellow male stall dweller was by tapping your foot
and swiping your hand along the floor? Just three days ago,

in DFW (Dallas/Fort Worth airport to you infrequent fly-ers), I was in the ladies' room performing the well-known automatic-faucet-activating gesture: frantically waving my hands, palm down, under the faucet, hoping to activate the sensor. Then, just before screaming, "Why don't they let us turn on our own damn faucets?" I realized that the hand waving could be a signal and that the lady at the adjacent sink could be an officer of the law. I hastily abandoned the effort to wash.

Once—and I admit this with some trepidation—I even consciously communicated with the occupant of an adja-cent stall. What I said was: "Could you pass me some toilet paper?" Then I reached down under the partition separat-ing us to collect the proffered paper. Now I realize it would have been wiser to leave the restroom unblotted, because a hand reaching into one's stall is surely a Craig-like signal.

For the last few years, since September 2001, my main air-port worry was that I might look or act like a terrorist. No exotic prints or dark eyeliner was my rule, though I had no hard evidence that female terrorists prefer them. No anxious glances at the uniformed personnel. No reading *Guns and Ammo*; instead carry *Real Simple* and *Martha Stewart Living*. No tantrums when the TSA confiscated my lip balm. But now I see that my efforts to look less like a terrorist might have made me look more like a, heaven forfend, lesbian.

Short of some undisclosed evidence that the 9/11 killers were closeted Wahhabist gays, you may wonder, as I do, why—with the "threat level" repeatedly elevated to an omi-nous orange—agents of the law are being deployed to detect people of alternative sexualities. Larry Craig was appre-hended by a man apparently consigned to spend his entire day on the can, watching for errant fingers. Possibly this fel-low has some intestinal issues that made this a necessary posting. But, sphincter control permitting, could he not have been more usefully employed, say, questioning passengers as to their willingness to blow themselves up to score some theological point?

This is what El Al, the Israeli airline, does, and it's believed to have the tightest security in the world. Its security people no doubt have bathroom breaks, but they spend a lot of their time on their feet too, talking to prospective passengers: Why are you traveling? Whom will you be seeing? Why aren't you carrying any tourist books? El Al doesn't rely on interviews alone, of course. They also confiscated my Baggie of peanuts, though who knows what havoc you could wreak with them.

The official justification for the security measures that have made air travel so scary is that they keep us safe—and, beyond that, free. But I'd feel safer and a whole lot freer if I didn't have to worry about accidentally impersonating a gay person. I'd feel freer still if I knew it didn't matter, travelwise, whether I was gay or straight. If lesbians want to cruise the ladies' rooms for quickies, which I very much doubt that they do, and if one of them should hit on me, which I find even more unlikely, I can always say, "Uh, not right now, I've got a plane to catch."

As for the fellow who unintentionally revealed the presence of the sex police in our airport restrooms: I'm hoping Larry Craig comes back and comes out. This will no doubt involve a tearful public renunciation of his past homophobia and a lifetime membership in the Log Cabin Republicans. But he'll meet plenty of guys, and in the end it will be so much easier not to have to pretend to take a leak every time he needs a little loving.

Let Them Eat Wedding Cake

C OMMITMENT ISN'T EASY FOR GUYS—WE ALL KNOW that—but the Bush administration took the traditional male ambivalence about marriage to giddy new heights. On the one hand, they wanted to ban gays from marrying. On the other hand, they were avidly promoting marriage among poor women—the straight ones, anyway.

Opponents of gay marriage are able to see some consistency here: Gay marriages must be stopped before they undermine the straight ones. But how married gays would go about wrecking heterosexual marriages has never been entirely clear: by moving in next door, inviting themselves over, and doing a devastating critique of the interior decorating?

It is equally unclear how marriage would cure poor women's No. 1 problem, which is poverty—unless, of course, the plan was to draft CEOs to marry recipients of TANF (Temporary Assistance to Needy Families). Left to themselves, most women end up marrying men of the same social class as their own, meaning—in the case of poverty-stricken women—blue-collar men. But that demographic group has seen a tragic decline in earnings in the last couple of decades. So I have been endeavoring to calculate just how many blue-collar men a TANF recipient needs to marry to lift her family out of poverty.

The answer turns out to be approximately 2.3, which is, strangely enough, illegal. Seeking clarity, I called the marriage maven Wade Horn at Health and Human Services. HHS is not "promoting" marriage, he told me, just providing "marriage education" for interested couples of limited means. The poor aren't being singled out for any insidious reason, he insisted; this is just a service they might otherwise lack. It could have been Pilates training or courses in orchid cultivation, was the implication, but for now it's marriage education. However, Horn is on the record proposing that Washington should "show it values marriage by rewarding those who choose it" with cash "marriage bonuses."

When I suggested that—with food pantries maxing out and shelters overflowing across the nation—poor women might have other priorities, Horn snapped back: "It's fine for you to make the decision on what low-income couples need." Silly old social-engineering-type liberal that I am, I had actually doubted that marriage education might be helpful to couples doomed to spend their married lives on separate cots in the shelter.

Besides, he went on, low-income people are eager for government-sponsored marriage education. Strangely, I've heard nothing about mobs of poor women picketing HHS daily, chanting: "What do we want? Marriage education! When do we want it? Now!" But maybe Wade Horn knows something I don't.

If marriage were a cure for poverty, I'd be the first to demand that the government spring for the limo and the wedding cake. But there is no evidence to that effect. Married couples are on average more prosperous than single mothers, but that doesn't mean marriage will lift the existing single mothers out of poverty. So what's the point of the administration's marriage meddling? Lisalyn Jacobs, who tracks TANF marriage policy at the women's group Legal Momentum, thinks that these mixed signals on marriage— OK for paupers, a no-no for gays—are part of a conservative effort to "change the subject to marriage." From, for example, Iraq.

But this may be too cynical an explanation. Quite possibly, the administration wants to ban gay marriage so that gay men can be drafted to marry TANF recipients. Think of all the problems that would solve and, if the Queer Eye stereotype holds true, how tastefully appointed those shelters will become.

Opportunities in Abstinence Training

I F THINGS ARE NOT WORKING OUT AS PLANNED, YOU might want to consider a career in the expanding field of abstinence education. The need is staggering: four out of five random people I surveyed on the street thought abstinence training is something you do with your midsection in the gym. Plus, unlike any of the rest of the coaching industry— career coaching, life coaching, sales training, etc.–this form of training is generously subsidized by the federal government, and has been since President Clinton signed the welfare reform bill of 1996, which provided abstinence training for impoverished women (though not, alas, for him).

It's not rocket science, either. In fact, there've been men in my life who were naturals at abstinence training without the slightest formal preparation: one renounced dental hygiene, another developed a passion for Frank Sinatra, leading me in each case to embrace abstinence without any regret. In yet another case, marriage alone was enough to induce that sanctified state.

Most people, though, require a bit of coaching to get into the abstinence training business, so I went to the Web site of WAIT Training to look at the sample curriculum for an abstinence course. The syllabus contained a lot about love, marriage, and STDs—none of it terribly technical, until I got to the part about how to explain the difference between the sexes, where the following demonstration was suggested: "Bring to class frozen waffles and a bowl of spaghetti noodles without sauce. Using these as visual aides, explain how research has found that men's brains are more like the waffle, in that their design allows them to more easily compartmentalize information. Women's minds, on the other hand are more interrelated due to increased brain connectors."

Maybe my spaghetti brain wasn't up to this challenge, but it did seem to imply that sex would involve a mixing of waffles and pasta, possibly with maple syrup for lubrication. Disgusting, yes, but no doubt a surefire recipe for abstinence.

My next step was to call Joneen Mackenzie, executive director of WAIT (which is an acronym for Why Am I Tempted?), to further pin down the requirements for becoming an abstinence trainer. Her program admits only college-educated people, but they can be of any age or sex. "Do they have to be abstinent themselves?" I asked. Not at all, she assured me, proudly confessing to being "like an animal" with her husband. How about gays? Well, yes, they could teach abstinence to gay teenagers. So, no barriers at all, and you can become a certified abstinence trainer after only two days of preparation.

There is, however, one shadow hanging over the abstinence training industry. A study commissioned by Congress revealed that it doesn't work: students exposed to abstinence training turn out to be no less likely to have sex than those who are not. Why, some wondered, should the federal government spend over $100 million on it annually? Mackenzie dismissed the study out of hand, saying it had been undertaken before serious abstinence education really got off the ground.

But there's a deeper problem with abstinence training as currently conducted: it's being wasted on kids. What better way to make sex a big deal than to tell kids they can't have any for years, and then only after spending $25,000 on champagne and bridesmaid's dresses? Also, kids have become more skeptical thanks to programs like DARE (Drug Abuse Resistance Education), the Web site of which currently proclaims that "cannabis can double chances of psychotic illness" and "just one cigarette can lead to addiction." If you've known marijuana smokers who are honor students, why would you believe that teen sex leads inevitably to heartbreak and oozing genital sores?

Here's my advice for the abstinence training industry and any novice abstinence trainers. First, leave the teenagers alone and focus on the vast neglected demographic of middle-aged and elderly people, including the married. Many of them think they just aren't getting any, so imagine how happy they will be to see their lifestyle affirmed as a noble, proactive choice! Think of the market for silver chastity rings (see www.silverringthing.com) in nursing homes and other long-term care facilities!

Second, and I realize that this may be more controversial, the abstinence training profession should be restricted to abstinent people. Would you undergo computer training with someone who hasn't touched a computer since 1987? Would you hire a flabby, out-of-shape personal fitness trainer? No, nor do I think you should study abstinence with someone who behaves "like an animal" in bed.

In any case, abstinence may be easier to achieve than you realize. Contrary to the assumptions of the framers of welfare reform, poverty—or at least sudden downward mobility—can lead to the rapid exit of significant others. You should welcome their departure and, if you are hetero-sexual, take it as an opportunity to withdraw into your own gender-appropriate Tupperware compartment—spaghetti or waffle.

Owning Up to Abortion

ABORTION IS LEGAL; IT'S JUST NOT SUPPOSED TO BE mentioned or acknowledged as an acceptable option. An article in the *New York Times* entitled "Television's Most Persistent Taboo" reported that a Viacom-owned channel refused to air the episodes of a soap opera in which the teenage heroine chooses to abort. Even *Six Feet Under*, which is fearless in its treatment of sexual diversity, burdened abortion with terrible guilt. Where are those "liberal media" when you need them?

You can blame a lot of folks—from media bigwigs to bishops—if we lose our reproductive rights, but it's the women who shrink from acknowledging their own abortions who really irk me. Increasingly, for example, the possibility of abortion is built right into the process of prenatal care. Testing for fetal defects can now detect more than 450 potentially fatal or debilitating conditions. Doctors may advise the screening tests, insurance companies often pay for them, and many couples (no hard numbers exist) are making the decision to abort their imperfect fetuses.

The trouble is, not all of the women who are exercising their right to choose in these cases are willing to admit that that's what they're doing. Kate Hoffman, for example, who aborted a fetus with Down's syndrome, was quoted in the *Times* as saying: "I don't look at it as though I had an abortion, even though that is technically what it is. There is a difference. I wanted this baby."

Or go to the Web site for A Heartbreaking Choice, an organization that provides support to women whose fetuses have been deemed defective, and you find "Mom" complaining of having to have her abortion in an ordinary clinic: "I resented the fact that I had to be there with all these girls that did not want their babies."

Kate and Mom: You've been through a hellish experience, but unless I'm missing something, you didn't want your babies either. A baby, yes, but not the particular baby you happened to be carrying.

The prejudice is widespread that a termination for medical reasons is somehow on a higher moral plane than a run-of-the-mill abortion. In a 1999 survey of Floridians, for example, 82 percent supported legal abortion in the case of birth defects, compared with about 40 percent in situations where the woman simply cannot afford to raise another child.

But what makes it morally more congenial to kill a particular "defective" fetus than to kill whatever fetus happens to come along, on an equal opportunity basis? Medically informed "terminations" are already catching heat from disability rights groups, and, indeed, some of the conditions for which people are currently choosing abortion—like deafness or dwarfism—seem a little sketchy to me. I'll still defend the right to choose abortion in these cases, even if it isn't the choice I'd make for myself.

It would be unfair, though, to pick on the women who are in denial about aborting diseased or "defective" fetuses. At least 30 million American women have had abortions since the procedure was legalized—which amounts to about 40 percent of American women—mostly for the kind of reasons that antichoicers dismiss as "convenience." Yet in a 2003 survey conducted by a prochoice group, only 30 percent of women were prochoice—suggesting that there are an appalling number who are willing to deny others the right that they once freely exercised themselves.

Honesty begins at home, so I should acknowledge that I had two abortions during my all-too-fertile years. You can call me a bad woman but not a bad mother. I was a dollar-a-word freelancer, my husband a warehouse worker, so it was all we could do to support the existing children at a fairly grubby lower-middle-class level. And when it comes to my children—the actual, extrauterine ones, that is—I was, and remain, a lioness.

Choice can be easy, as it was in my case, or truly agonizing. But assuming the fetal position is not an appropriate response. Sartre called this "bad faith," meaning something worse than duplicity—a fundamental denial of freedom and the responsibility that it entails. Time to take your thumbs out of your mouths, ladies, and speak up for your rights. The freedoms that we exercise but do not defend, or even acknowledge, are easily taken away.

How Banning Gay Marriage
Will Destroy the Family

SOMEONE HAS TO SAY IT: A CONSTITUTIONAL AMEND-
ment banning gay marriage will destroy the American
family and all the sex-related "values" our brethren on the
religious right hold so dear. How will it do so? By creating
an irresistible demand for a constitutional amendment banning *heterosexual* marriage.

The logic is clear. Since the Supreme Court ruled in
Lawrence v. Texas (in 2003) that antisodomy laws are uncon-
stitutional, it's been legal for gays to have sex. Add to that a
ban on gay marriage and you will create a special class of
people—gays and lesbians—who are free to have all the sex
they want, as long as it's outside of marriage.

This is bound to lead to grumbling among the hetero-
sexual population, even a certain amount of gay envy. Het-
erosexuals will start saying: "How come we're supposed to
get married if we want to have sex? How come homosexu-
als get all the breaks?"

True, most of the demand for a constitutional amendment banning straight marriage will come from the commitment-phobic eighteen-to-thirty-six-year-old male demographic, but this happens to be the most influential demographic in the land. Its tastes determine what movies are made, what we see on TV, and whether we can find sneakers that don't look like rubberized platform shoes. If the eighteen-to-thirty-six-year-old male demographic demands a ban on hetero-sexual marriage, you can bet that the right-leaning politicians will change their tune faster than you can say "Dick Cheney's daughter."

Instead of bashing gays for their insidious "lifestyle," the politicians will start beating up on them for their "special privileges"—the right to party all night until well into your fifties, the right to blow off a partner as soon as he or she starts carping about closet space, and so on. Straight young men will tire of trying to pass as gay as soon as the conversation turns to children. They'll run into the streets shouting, "Freedom from marriage for all!"

And if a ban on gay marriage doesn't succeed in actually destroying the American family, it will certainly do a great deal to annoy the American family. Face it, there are no "heterosexual families" or "gay families." These days, any extended family that doesn't contain at least one gay couple just hasn't extended itself very far. There are gays and gay couples caring for elderly (usually straight) parents or children, and gays who bring the green bean casserole to mixed-sexual-orientation Thanksgivings. In short, gays are embedded in "the American family," and anyone who messes with them is messing with that noble institution.

Families have a stake in marriage if only because it's an occasion for a wedding, meaning a chance to dress up, drink too much, and flirt with your cousin's ex-husband. If gays can't marry, that's one less wedding per extended family, and that, I say, is too high a price to pay.

You still don't like the idea of gay marriage? Then, as my friend the economist Julianne Malveaux says: Don't marry a gay person. Case closed, problem solved.

Do Women Need a Viagra?

THERE'S NO END OF SPECIES-THREATENING DISEASE, with TB, AIDS, bird flu, and MRSA, but what's got Big Pharma working overtime is the female orgasm. And now that the drug companies are on the verge of a major new breakthrough—a Viagra-type drug for women—feminists are in a major snit. One faction is muttering that the drug companies are sexist for taking so long to find a cure for female sexual dysfunction (FSD) while the fix for its male counterpart, erectile dysfunction, has been available for over five years. Others, like sex expert Shere Hite, are already denouncing the drug companies for "cynical money grabbing"—that is, creating a disease in order to market a pill or a patch.

On the Viagra-envying side of the debate are plenty of women who find their libidos drained by surgery, menopause, crying infants, or overwork. Plus, there is a significant minority still seeking the zipless interaction popularized by Erica Jong in *Fear of Flying*: skip the relationship, the candlelight, and the wine, and cut to the chase. I know at least one respectable grandma who is preparing for the advent of a female Viagra by stocking up on batteries for her vibrator.

Still, I wonder: is there really a need for an orgasm-promoting drug for women? The drug companies like to cite a study suggesting that 43 percent of American women suffer from FSD, which would make the disorder more than ten times as prevalent as breast cancer or AIDS, though surely a bit more bearable. But detractors point out that in the study women were judged to have FSD for answering yes to any one of seven questions, such as whether they had experienced difficulty with lubrication or sometimes lacked desire. Perhaps the more amazing conclusion is that 57 percent of American women seemed to be ready to party at the drop of a hat.

You might also ask, if FSD is so widespread, why Viagra is now about as popular as vitamin C among all those male sex partners. To judge from the billion-dollar market for Viagra, no man can count on slipping peacefully into impotence. Who's behind the massive use of Viagra, if not an army of FSD-free girlfriends and wives? Even reliably potent men are now indulging, says the *New York Times*, thanks to the influence of *Sex and the City*, which has suggested "a Samantha complex, a fear of wilting in the face of a new wave of sexually empowered women." Perhaps the drug companies are trying to promote an arms race between pumped-up Viagra poppers and chemically Samantha-ized women?

This wouldn't be the first time that the medical profession was caught inventing a disease to go with the cure in hand. In the 1990s plastic surgeons discovered "micromastia," a syndrome characterized solely by small breasts and conveniently curable with silicone implants. A century and some years ago, doctors detected an epidemic of "hysteria" among affluent women, manifested by hundreds of unrelated symptoms and requiring constant medical attention.

Furthermore, it's not clear that FSD, to the extent it exists, can be vanquished with a pill. Unlike male sexuality, female sexuality isn't just a matter of plumbing. Context matters more than it seems to in men—along with emotion, fantasy, and, yes, candlelight—so that anyone afflicted with FSD might do better to claim some leisure in her life and work on rekindling the romance. Of course, the same may be true for the Viagra-taking sex, a surprising 50 percent of whom fail to renew their prescriptions.

Finally, as psychiatrist Leonore Tiefer argues, there's something deeply creepy about the medicalization of sexuality, male and female. Once there's a drug to prescribe, doctors will feel the need to establish "norms"—say, two orgasms a week—and women who fall short are bound to feel inadequate, unfeminine, even pathological. Better, Tiefer thinks, for them to seek more satisfying relationships or more inspiring partners than rely on a pill for their thrills.

Still, if there's a possibility of a female version of Viagra, I say, Get it to the market fast. Only make that the black market, or at least over the counter. Let's circumvent the medical profession, with all its profoundly off-turning talk about disorders and norms, and appropriate the new drug for purely recreational use, just as men are doing with Viagra. Sure, we need dashing partners and the leisurely evenings in which to enjoy them, but these improvements could be years in coming, if ever. In the meantime, my guru is Cyndi Lauper, with her revolutionary dictum: Girls just wanna have fun. If Big Pharma comes up with something to advance that agenda, bring it on.

A Uterus Is Not a Substitute
for a Conscience

E VEN PEOPLE WE MIGHT HAVE THOUGHT WERE IMPER-
vious to shame, like the secretary of defense, admit
that the photos of abuse in Iraq's Abu Ghraib prison turned
their stomachs.

To me, as a feminist, the photos did something else: they
broke my heart. I had no illusions about the US mission in
Iraq—whatever exactly it is—but it turns out that I did have
some illusions about women.

Of the seven US soldiers charged with sickening forms
of abuse in Abu Ghraib, three were women: Specialist
Megan Ambuhl, Private First Class Lynndie England, and
Specialist Sabrina Harman.

It was Harman we saw smiling an impish little smile and
giving the thumbs-up sign from behind a pile of hooded,
naked Iraqi men—as if to say, "Hi, Mom, here I am in Abu
Ghraib!" It was England we saw with a naked Iraqi man on
a leash. If you were doing PR for Al Qaeda, you couldn't

have staged a better picture to galvanize misogynist Islamic fundamentalists around the world.

Here, in these photos from Abu Ghraib, you have everything that the Islamic fundamentalists believe characterizes Western culture, all nicely arranged in one hideous image—imperial arrogance, sexual depravity, . . . and gender equality.

Maybe I shouldn't have been so shocked. We know that good people can do terrible things under the right circumstances. This is what psychologist Stanley Milgram found in his famous experiments in the 1960s. In all likelihood, Ambuhl, England, and Harman are not congenitally evil people. They are working-class women who wanted an education and knew that the military could be a stepping-stone in that direction. Once they had joined, they wanted to fit in.

And I also shouldn't be surprised because I never believed that women were innately gentler and less aggressive than men. Like most other feminists, I have supported full opportunity for women within the military (1) because I knew women could fight and (2) because the military is one of the few options around for low-income young people.

Although I opposed the 1991 Persian Gulf War, I was proud of our servicewomen and delighted that their presence irked their Saudi hosts. Secretly, I hoped that the presence of women would over time change the military, making it more respectful of other people and cultures, more capable of genuine peacekeeping. That's what I thought, but I don't think that anymore.

A certain kind of feminism, or perhaps I should say a certain kind of feminist naiveté, died in Abu Ghraib. It was a feminism that saw men as the perpetual perpetrators, women as the perpetual victims, and male sexual violence

against women as the root of all injustice. Rape has repeatedly been an instrument of war and, to some feminists, it
was beginning to look as if war was an extension of rape.
There seemed to be at least some evidence that male sexual
sadism was connected to our species' tragic propensity for
violence. That was before we had seen female sexual
sadism in action.

But it's not just the theory of this naive feminism that was
wrong. So was its strategy and vision for change. That strategy and vision rested on the assumption, implicit or stated
outright, that women were morally superior to men. We had
a lot of debates over whether it was biology or conditioning
that gave women the moral edge—or simply the experience
of being a woman in a sexist culture. But the assumption of
superiority, or at least of a lesser inclination toward cruelty
and violence, was more or less beyond debate. After all,
women do most of the caring work in our culture and in
polls are consistently less inclined toward war than men.

I'm not the only one wrestling with that assumption.
Mary Jo Melone, a columnist for the *St. Petersburg Times*,
wrote: "I can't get that picture of England [pointing at a
hooded Iraqi man's genitals] out of my head because this is
not how women are expected to behave. Feminism taught
me 30 years ago that not only had women gotten a raw deal
from men, we were morally superior to them."

If that assumption had been accurate, then all we would
have had to do to make the world a better place—kinder, less
violent, more just—would have been to assimilate into what
had been, for so many centuries, the world of men. We
would fight so that women could become the generals,
CEOs, senators, professors, and opinion makers—and that
was really the only fight we had to undertake. Because once
they gained power and authority, once they had achieved a

critical mass within the institutions of society, women would naturally work for change. That's what we thought, even if we thought it unconsciously—and it's just not true. Women can do the unthinkable.

You can't even argue, in the case of Abu Ghraib, that the problem was that there just weren't enough women in the military hierarchy to stop the abuses. The prison was directed by a woman, General Janis Karpinski. The top US intelligence officer in Iraq, who also was responsible for reviewing the status of detainees before their release, was Major General Barbara Fast. And the US official ultimately responsible for managing the occupation of Iraq was Condoleezza Rice. Like Donald H. Rumsfeld, she ignored repeated reports of abuse and torture until the undeniable photographic evidence emerged.

What we have learned from Abu Ghraib, once and for all, is that a uterus is not a substitute for a conscience. This doesn't mean gender equality isn't worth fighting for for its own sake. It is. If we believe in democracy, then we believe in a woman's right to do and achieve whatever men can do and achieve, even the bad things. It's just that gender equality cannot, all by itself, bring about a just and peaceful world.

In fact, we have to realize, in all humility, that the kind of feminism based on an assumption of female moral superiority is not only naive; it is also a lazy and self-indulgent form of feminism. Self-indulgent because it assumes that a victory for a woman—a promotion, a college degree, the right to serve alongside men in the military—is by its very nature a victory for all of humanity. And lazy because it assumes that we have only one struggle—the struggle for gender equality—when in fact we have many more.

The struggles for peace and social justice and against

imperialist and racist arrogance cannot, I am truly sorry to say, be folded into the struggle for gender equality.

What we need is a tough new kind of feminism with no illusions. Women do not change institutions simply by assimilating into them, only by consciously deciding to fight for change. We need a feminism that teaches a woman to say no—not just to the date rapist or overly insistent boyfriend but, when necessary, to the military or corporate hierarchy within which she finds herself.

In short, we need a kind of feminism that aims not just to assimilate into the institutions that men have created over the centuries but to infiltrate and transform them.

To cite an old and far from naive feminist saying: "If you think equality is the goal, your standards are too low." It is not enough to be equal to men, when the men are acting like beasts. It is not enough to assimilate. We need to create a world worth assimilating into.

Who's Wrecking the Family?

I WAS IN THE ATLANTA AIRPORT, CRUISING A BOOKSTORE, when this catchy title leaped out at me: *Women Who Make the World Worse—and How Their Radical Feminist Assault Is Ruining Our Schools, Families, Military, and Sports.* Since the author is Fox News pundit Kate O'Beirne, I indulged my vanity and looked up my name in the index. There I was, right up front on page 4, credited with ruining our families.

If O'Beirne had done a little more research, she might have found me responsible for wrecking our military and schools as well. But I can't complain: destroying the family is a hefty accomplishment all by itself.

This isn't the first time I'd gotten right-wing attention as a home wrecker. Back in the midnineties, James Dobson's Focus on the Family described me as a woman who'd dedicated her life to the destruction of the American family, in more or less those words. Partly this is just the right-wing translation of the word *feminist.* Some of you may recall Pat Robertson's attack on feminism during the controversy over the Equal Rights Amendment in the eighties. Feminists, he said, busy themselves becoming lesbians, killing their children, and advancing Marxism—a formidable agenda, to say the least, especially if your children are fast on their feet.

But partly I brought these accusations down on myself. In an essay in *Time* magazine, I once proposed that we replace the slippery institution of marriage with a binding, lifelong contract between adults to take responsibility for their children. The sexual attraction between two adults is not, I reasoned, a firm enough basis for a family, but the responsibility for children should remain rock solid and indissoluble, no matter how much the grown-ups stray. And in my book, children come first.

As it happened, what had brought me to Atlanta was not a trip to a convention of lesbian Marxist child killers. I was returning from a holiday spent with my son and his girlfriend and my nephew and his wife, and I was rushing home because I was eager to rejoin my granddaughters (ages six and three), who are the light of my life. News of the Dobson attack had hit at a similar moment: I was returning from a visit to my grandmother and an ailing aunt in Iowa. My job may be to "destroy the American family," but I've never managed to destroy a single family member, even one of the more irritating ones.

If anyone is "ruining" the American family, it's all the employers who refuse to recognize that their employees have family responsibilities as well as jobs. I'm thinking of two categories of employers that often overlap: those who don't pay enough for their employees to live on, thus forcing them to work second jobs, and those who abuse their salaried employees with expectations of ten or more hours of work per day. There are more and more such antifamily employers because, as economist Juliet Schor showed in her book *The Overworked American*, our hours of work have risen sharply since the seventies and now surpass even those of the famously workaholic Japanese.

There was a telling moment when I was interviewing a laid-off finance guy. He complained to me that his last boss hadn't given him any "work-life balance," even though he had specifically requested it. I was baffled: "work-life balance" is something you have to ask for—a kind of "special need"?

All sorts of things suffer when work expands to fill evenings and weekends—health, for example, and citizenly participation. How can you frame an opinion on the issues if you never get a chance to read or have discussions with friends? But family—and especially children—take the worst hit. It's just not possible to be a responsible and responsive parent or spouse if your job(s) leave you with barely enough time to shower.

To get back to Kate O'Beirne: Will you help me save the family by joining me in a campaign for adequate wages and a return to the concept of the eight-hour day?

If not, let's at least fight fair. You get out your photos of your grandkids (if any) and I'll get out mine.

Bonfire of the Princesses

CONTRARY TO THE RUMORS I HAVE BEEN TRYING TO spread for some time, Disney Princess products are not contaminated with lead. More careful analysis shows that the entire product line—books, DVDs, ball gowns, necklaces, toy cell phones, toothbrush holders, T-shirts, lunch boxes, backpacks, wallpaper, sheets, stickers, etc.—is saturated with a particularly potent time-release form of the date-rape drug.

We cannot blame China this time, because the drug is in the concept, which was spawned in the Disney studios. Before 2000, the Princesses were just the separate, disunited heroines of Disney animated films—Snow White, Cinderella, Ariel, Aurora, Pocahontas, Jasmine, Belle, and Mulan. Then Disney's Andy Mooney got the idea of bringing the gals together in a team. With a wave of the wand ($10.99 at Target, tiara included), they were all elevated to royal status and set loose on the world as an imperial cabal, and they have since busied themselves achieving global

domination. Today, there is no little girl in the wired industrial world who does not seek to display her allegiance to
the pink-and-purple-clad Disney dynasty.

Disney likes to think of the Princesses as role models, but
what a sorry bunch of wusses they are. Typically, they spend
much of their time in captivity or a coma, waking up only
when a Prince comes along and kisses them. The most
striking exception is Mulan, who dresses as a boy to fight in
the army, but—like the other Princess of color, Pocahontas—
she lacks full Princess status and does not warrant a line of
tiaras and gowns. Otherwise the Princesses have no ambi-
tions and no marketable skills, although both Snow White
and Cinderella are good at housecleaning.

And what could they aspire to, beyond landing a Prince?
In Princessland, the only career ladder leads from baby-faced
adolescence to a position as an evil enchantress, stepmother,
or witch. Snow White's wicked stepmother is consumed with
envy of her stepdaughter's beauty; the sea witch Ursula cov-
ets Ariel's lovely voice; Cinderella's stepmother exploits the
girl's cheap, uncomplaining labor. No need for complicated
witch-hunting techniques—pin prickings and dunkings—in
Princessland. All you have to look for is wrinkles.

Feminist parents gnash their teeth. For this their little
girls gave up Dora, who bounds through the jungle saving
baby jaguars, whose mother is an archeologist, and whose
adventures don't involve smoochy rescues by Diego? There
was drama in Dora's life, too, and the occasional bad actor
like Swiper the fox. Even Barbie looks like a suffragette
compared with Disney's Belle. So what's the appeal of the
pink-tulle Princess cult?

Seen from the witchy end of the female life cycle, the
Princesses exert their pull through a dark and undeniable
eroticism. They're sexy little wenches, for one thing. Snow

White has gotten slimmer and bustier over the years; Ariel wears nothing but a bikini top (though, admittedly, she is half fish). In faithful imitation, the three-year-old in my life flounces around with her tiara askew and her Princess gown sliding off her shoulder, looking for all the world like a London socialite after a hard night of cocaine and booze. Then she demands a poison apple and falls to the floor in a beautiful swoon. Pass the Rohypnol-laced margarita, please.

It may be old-fashioned to say so, but sex—and especially some middle-aged man's twisted version thereof—doesn't belong in the pre-K playroom. Children are going to discover it soon enough, but they've got to do so on their own.

There's a reason, after all, we're generally more disgusted by sexual abusers than by adults who inflict mere violence on children: we sense that sexual abuse more deeply messes with a child's mind. One's sexual inclinations—straightforward or kinky, active or passive, heterosexual or homosexual—should be free to develop without adult intervention or manipulation. Hence our harshness toward the kind of sexual predators who leer at kids and offer candy. But Disney, which also owns ABC, Lifetime, ESPN, A&E, and Miramax, is rewarded with $4 billion a year for marketing the masochistic Princess cult and its endlessly proliferating paraphernalia.

No parent can stand up against this alone. Try to ban the Princesses from your home, and you might as well turn yourself in to Child Protective Services before the little girls get on their Princess cell phones. No, the only way to topple royalty is through a mass uprising of the long-suffering serfs. Assemble with your neighbors and make a holiday bonfire out of all that plastic and tulle! March on Disney World with pitchforks held high!

FALSE GODS

The Secret of Mass Delusion

THE LEADERS OF DELTA ZETA—THE SORORITY THAT made national news by expelling all overweight and nonwhite members from its Depauw University chapter—must have read *The Secret.* In this runaway self-help best seller, Rhonda Byrne advises that you can keep your weight down by avoiding the sight of fat people: "If you see people who are overweight, do not observe them, but immediately switch your mind to the picture of you in your perfect body and feel it." Don't worry about calories; just get rid of that 150-pound sorority sister down the hall.

Here's The Secret, in case you missed it: you can have anything you want simply by visualizing it intensely enough through a mysterious "law of attraction." I don't have to write this article; I can simply visualize it already written—or could, if I'd bothered to read the whole book and finish the DVD. To be fair to Byrne, she does not suggest avoiding nonwhite people; in fact, one of the teachers of The Secret whom she cites is the African American motivational speaker Lisa Nichols. The Delta Zeta leaders probably just thought: Why take a chance?

Can you really get anything you want through the law of attraction? It may not work as smoothly as its advocates promise. Take the case of Esther Hicks, spirit channeler, motivational speaker, and coauthor of a book entitled *The Law of Attraction*. Byrne had told Hicks she would have a starring role in the DVD of *The Secret*, but her face was never shown in the film's first cut (although her voice, channeling a group of spirits called "Abraham," was used throughout). Hicks was furious and demanded that her voice, or Abraham's, also be excised from the DVD, which has now sold about 1.5 million copies.

Possibly Hicks was just too fat for the film, or at least too dowdy. It's hard to judge her weight from a photo in the *New York Times* that shows her seated—eyes closed in channeling mode—inside her $1.4 million bus. But just underneath is a photo of a sylphlike Byrnes frolicking on a beach in a fur-trimmed jacket. From a Delta Zeta perspective, whom would you rather look at?

Hicks says she is not going to sue, and why should she? She could just use the law of attraction to reinsert herself back into the DVD. Or to deflect Byrne's profits into her own bank account. Or to take off fifteen pounds and have them padded onto Byrne's tiny waist.

If a leading proponent of the law of attraction cannot control a little thing like a DVD with her thoughts, then why are millions of Americans spending good money to find out how to use that law to control the entire universe? The scary thing is that the subscribers to the law aren't just a bunch of wistful, isolated misfits. Read the reviews of the DVD of *The Secret* and you find that companies are beginning to impose it on their employees. An N. Van Buskirk writes: "I was presented this DVD at work and I found it disturbing. A gimmick to say the least, but the real issue is that I felt like I was being indoctrinated into a cult—I had to leave about half-way through." However, Steven E. Cramer, an employer, reports that "I had my sales staff watch 'The Secret,' and saw an immediate jump in morale, goals and production."

Check out the credentials of the "teachers" enlisted in The Secret. Most are well-known motivational speakers who claim to instruct such business heavyweights as financial advisers, developers, and a "master marketer." One of The Secret's teachers, Denis Waitley, includes on his Web site testimonials from Merrill Lynch, WorldCom, 3M, Dell, and IBM, among many others.

Well, here's a little secret I'd like to share, channeled to me by Einstein, Newton, and thousands of Enlightenment thinkers: when the leaders of a major economy lapse into mysticism and come to believe they can accomplish things through their mental vibrations, without lifting a finger, then it's time to start thinking about going into subsistence farming on a remote compound in Idaho. I'll have the DVD out in no time.

Who Moved My Ability
to Reason?

THERE THEY ARE, MASSED IN EVERY BOOKSTORE, THEIR titles lunging out to slap you in the face. Some are straight-out commands, like *First, Break All the Rules* and *Now, Discover Your Strengths*. Others pose quirky metaphorical questions: *How Full Is Your Bucket?* or *Who Moved My Cheese?* Several of them trumpet forth a kind of numerological majesty: *The 8th Habit, The Five Dysfunctions of a Team*. All lay claim to the almost infinite territory of "work and life," as in the *Cheese* subtitle, *An Amazing Way to Deal with Change in Your Work and in Your Life*. Clearly you are not in the literature section, or even ordinary diet and mood-boosting self-help; this is the bustling genre of business success books, descended from Dale Carnegie's mid-twentieth-century oeuvre and ready, if only you believe, to transform you into a CEO now.

Fortunately, these books are easy to read, since they're directed at an audience more familiar with PowerPoints than Proust. Few words clutter the pages of Spencer Johnson's mega–best seller, *Who Moved My Cheese?*, or his follow-up book, *The Present*, whose covers are emblazoned with a kind of stamp that contains the phrase "a gem–small and valuable." In place of words, one often finds graphics, like the little buckets that help fill the pages of *How Full Is Your Bucket?* The caption on the book tells us: "Everyone has an invisible bucket. We are at our best when our buckets are overflowing–and at our worst when they are empty." Even the unusually prolix four hundred pages of *The 8th Habit* are heavily padded with graphlike diagrams, including one depicting a wrinkled sine wave–or perhaps it's a mountain–labeled "Passion." The mountain rises from a sea swimming with "positive" words like "hope," "synergistic," "fun," and "motivating."

The few words that do appear in these books are likely to be bolded, bulleted, or boxed. Lists are unavoidable. *Now, Discover Your Strengths* includes a list with thirty-four possible strength-related "themes," from "achiever" to "maximizer" to "woo." Chapters are often embedded with simple exercises you can perform at home, like this one from *Secrets of the Millionaire Mind*: "Place your hand on your heart and say, . . . 'I admire rich people!' 'I bless rich people!' 'I love rich people!' 'And I'm going to be one of those rich people too!'" In some cases, the author seems ready to abandon print altogether, ending his book with instructions to visit his Web site, purchase his nonbook products, or attend his motivational seminars (and they are, in the current batch of business success books, always "his"). For members of the postreading generation, *How Full Is Your Bucket?* and *The 8th Habit* tuck in a convenient CD.

But why read these books at all? Herewith are "The Five Essential Principles of Business Success Books," conveniently condensed for consumption in five minutes or less.

Yes, they overlap and sometimes contradict one another. No, the headings are not parallel, some being nouns, some adjectives, and some entire sentences. Welcome to the genre!

The 24/7 Happy Hour. Be positive, upbeat, and perky at all times. Once, the job of corporate functionaries was to make things happen. Today, their mission is apparently to keep their colleagues company in the office. As *How Full Is Your Bucket?* asserts, "Ninety-nine out of every 100 people report that they want to be around more positive people." Every book in the genre enjoins a relentless positivity of outlook. In the *Tuesdays with Morrie*–like fable of *The Present,* the anonymous "young man" chirps to the wise "old man," "So, if what I believe and do today is positive, I help create a better tomorrow!"

In fact, negative thoughts—as toward the boss who laid you off or passed you over for a promotion—will not only be visible to your comrades but "can be harmful to your health and might even shorten your life span." If you happen to be downsized, right-sized, or outsourced again, just grin and bear your smiley face to the next potential employer, as the happy folks in *We Got Fired! . . . And It's the Best Thing That Ever Happened to Us* advise.

Avoid Victimism and Anyone Who Indulges in It. People who fail at being positive—and dwell morbidly on their last demotion or downsizing, for example—easily fall into what *The 8th Habit* diagnoses as "the mind-set of victimism and culture of blame." Avoid them, even though "it's very easy to hang out and share suffering with people who are committed to lose." Poor people, we discover in *Secrets of the Millionaire Mind,* are that way because they "choose to play the role of the victim." Avoid them, too.

Masters of the Universe. Being positive and upbeat not

only improves your health and popularity, it actually changes the world. Yes, your thoughts can alter the physical universe, which, according to *Secrets of the Millionaire Mind*, "is akin to a big mail-order department" in which you "'order' what you get by sending energetic messages out to the universe." The author ascribes this wisdom to the law of attraction, which was explained scientifically in the 2001 book *The Ultimate Secret to Getting Absolutely Everything You Want*. Thoughts exert a gravitational-type force on the world, so that "whenever you think something, the thought immediately attracts its physical equivalent." If you think money—in a totally urgent, focused, and positive way, of course—it will come flying into your pockets.

The Mice Come Out Ahead. Although the plot of *Who Moved My Cheese?* centers on two tiny, maze-dwelling, cheese-dependent people named Hem and Haw, there are also two subsidiary characters, both mice. When the cheese is moved, the tiny people waste time ranting and raving "at the injustice of it all," as the book's title suggests. But the mice just scurry off to locate an alternative cheese source. They prevail, we learn, because they "kept life simple. They didn't overanalyze or overcomplicate things." In the mysteriously titled *QBQ! The Question behind the Question*, we are told that questions beginning with "who" or "why" are symptoms of "victim thinking." Happily, rodents are less prone to it than humans. That may be why we never learn the identity of the Cheese Mover; the "who" question reveals a dangerous human tendency to "overanalyze," which could lead you to look upward, resentfully, toward the C-suites where the true Masters of the Universe dwell.

Passionate. According to *The 8th Habit*, in the old days it was good enough to be effective. But "being effective ... is no longer optional in today's world—it's the price of entry to the playing field." The endlessly churning, cutthroat twenty-first-century business world demands greatness—which means being not only enthusiastic but also passionate about your work. Presumably, you will pull all-nighters, neglect your family—whatever it takes. And when you do lose your job, you will embrace your next one—in, say, modular building construction—with the same raging passion for greatness.

There you have it, the five highly condensed secrets of business success. If you find them immoral, delusional, or insulting to the human spirit, you should humbly consider the fact that, to judge from the blurbs on the backs of these books, they have won the endorsement of numerous actual CEOs of prominent companies. Maybe the books tell us what these fellows want their underlings to believe. Be more like mice, for example. Or—and this is the truly scary possibility—maybe the principles embody what the CEOs themselves believe, and it is in fact the delusional, the immoral, and the verbally challenged who are running the show.

All Together Now

THEIR FACES LONG WITH DISAPPROVAL, THE ANCHORS announced that the reason for the war in Iraq had finally been uncovered by the Senate Intelligence Committee, and it was "groupthink," not to mention "collective groupthink." It sounds so kinky and un-American, like something that might go on in a North Korean stadium. But supposedly intelligent, morally upstanding people had been indulging in it right in Langley, Virginia.

This is a surprise? Groupthink has become as American as apple pie and prisoner abuse; in fact, it's hard to find any thinking these days that doesn't qualify for the prefix "group." Our standardized-test-driven schools reward the right answer, not the unsettling question. Our corporate culture prides itself on individualism, but it's the "team player" with the fixed smile who gets to be employee of the month. In our political culture, the most crushing rebuke is to call someone "out of step with the American people." Zip your lips, is the universal message, and get with the program.

The 2004 remake of *The Stepford Wives* didn't have anything coherent to say about gender politics: Men are the oppressors? Women are the oppressors? Or maybe just Glenn Close? But it did play to the fantasy, more widespread than I'd realized, that if you were to rip off the face of the person sitting in the next cubicle, you'd find nothing but circuit boards underneath.

I trace the outbreak of droidlike conformity to the aftermath of 9/11, when groupthink became the official substitute for patriotism and we began to run out of surfaces for affixing American flags. Bill Maher lost his job for pointing out that, whatever else they were, the 9/11 terrorists weren't cowards, prompting press secretary Ari Fleischer to warn that Americans "need to watch what they say." Never mind that somewhere in his oeuvre, Sun Tzu, so beloved by the leadership industry, says that while it's soothing to underestimate the enemy, it's often fatal, too.

And what was that group thinking in Abu Ghraib? True, the accused guards were apparently encouraged to soften up their charges for interrogation, just as the operatives at Langley were pelted with White House demands for some plausible casus belli. But the alarming thing is how few soldiers demurred, and how many got caught up in the fun of it.

Societies throughout history have recognized the hazards of groupthink and made arrangements to guard against it. The shaman, the wise woman, and similar figures all represent institutionalized outlets for alternative points of view. In the European carnival tradition, a "king of fools" was permitted to mock the authorities, at least for a day or two. In some cultures, people resorted to vision quests or hallucinogens—anything to get out of the box. Because, while the capacity for groupthink is an endearing part of our legacy as social animals, it's also a common precondition for self-destruction. Thousands of soldiers and civilians have died because the CIA was so eager to go along with the emperor's delusion that he was actually wearing clothes.

Instead of honoring groupthink resisters, we subject them to insult and abuse. Sergeant Samuel Provance III has been shunned by fellow soldiers since speaking out against the torture at Abu Ghraib, in addition to losing his security clearance and being faced with a possible court-martial. A fellow Abu Ghraib whistle-blower, Specialist Joseph Darby, was praised by the brass but has had to move to an undisclosed location to avoid grassroots retaliation.

The list goes on. Sibel Edmonds lost her job at the FBI for complaining about mistranslations of terror-related documents from the Arabic. Jesselyn Radack was driven out of her post at the Justice Department for objecting to the treatment of "the American Taliban" John Walker Lindh and then harassed by John Ashcroft's enforcers at her next job. As Fred Alford, a political scientist who studies the fate of whistle-blowers, puts it: "We need to understand in this 'land of the free and home of the brave' that most people are scared to death. About 50 percent of all whistle-blowers lose their jobs, about half of those lose their homes, and half of those people lose their families."

This nation was not founded by habitual groupthinkers. But it stands a fair chance of being destroyed by them.

The Faith Factor

O F ALL THE LOATHSOME SPECTACLES WE ENDURED
after Bush's 2004 election, none was more repulsive
than that of Democrats conceding the "moral values" edge to
the party that brought us Guantanamo. The cries for Democrats to overcome their "out-of-touchness" and embrace the
predominant faith all dodged the full horror of the situation:
a criminal was enabled to continue his bloody work with the
help, in no small part, of self-identified Christians.

With their craven, breast-beating response to Bush's
electoral triumph, leading Democrats only demonstrated
how out of touch they really were with the religious trans-
formation of America. Where secular-type liberals and cen-
trists go wrong is in categorizing religion as a form of
"irrationality," akin to spirituality, sports mania, and emotion generally. They fail to see that the current "Christian-
ization" of parts of America bears no resemblance to the
Great Revival of the late eighteenth century, an ecstatic
movement that filled the fields of Virginia with the rolling,

shrieking, and jerking bodies of the revived. In contrast, today's right-leaning Christian churches represent a vastly diluted Calvinist tradition in which even speaking in tongues, if it occurs at all, has been increasingly routinized and restricted to the pastor. No, what these churches have to offer, in addition to intangibles like eternal salvation, is concrete, material assistance. They have become an alternative welfare state, whose support rests not only on "faith" but also on the loyalty of the grateful recipients.

Drive out from Washington to the Virginia suburbs, for example, and you'll find the McLean Bible Church, spiritual home of Senator James Inhofe and other prominent right-wingers, still hopping on a weekday night. Dozens of families and teenagers enjoy a low-priced dinner in the cafeteria; a hundred unemployed people meet for prayer and job tips at the "Career Ministry"; divorced and abused women gather in support groups. Among its many services, MBC distributes free clothing to ten thousand poor people a year, helped start an inner-city ministry for at-risk youth in D.C., and operates a "special needs" ministry for disabled children.

MBC is a megachurch with a parking garage that could serve a medium-sized airport, but many smaller evangelical churches offer a similar array of services—child care, after-school programs, ESL lessons, help in finding a job, not to mention the occasional cash handout. A woman I met in Minneapolis gave me her strategy for surviving bouts of destitution: "First, you find a church." A trailer park dweller in Grand Rapids told me that he often turned to his church for help with the rent. Got a drinking problem, a vicious spouse, a wayward child, a bill due? Find a church. The closest analogy to America's bureaucratized evangelical movement is Hamas, which draws in poverty-stricken Palestinians through its own miniature welfare state.

Nor is the local business elite neglected by the evangelicals. Evangelical churches are vital centers of "networking," where the carwash owner can schmooze with the bank's loan officer. Some churches offer regular Christian businessmen's "fellowship lunches," where religious testimonies are given and business cards traded, along with jokes aimed at Democrats and gays.

Mainstream, even liberal, churches also provide a range of services, from soup kitchens to support groups. What makes the typical evangelical social welfare effort sinister is its implicit—and sometimes not so implicit—linkage to a program for the destruction of public and secular services. The connecting code words are *abortion* and *gay marriage*: to vote for the candidate who opposes these supposed moral atrocities, as the Christian Coalition and so many churches strongly advise, is also to vote against public housing subsidies, child care, and expanded public forms of health insurance. While Hamas operates in the absence of a welfare state, the Christian right advances by attacking the one we have.

Of course, a faith-based social welfare strategy only accelerates the downward spiral toward theocracy. Not only do the right-leaning evangelical churches offer their own, shamelessly proselytizing social services, not only do they attack candidates who favor expanded public services, but they stand to gain public money by doing so. It is this dangerous positive feedback loop, and not any new spiritual or moral dimension of American life, that the Democrats have failed to comprehend: the evangelical church-based welfare system is being fed by the deliberate destruction of the secular welfare state.

Democrats should not be flirting with faith but articulating poverty and war as the urgent moral issues they are.

Jesus is on our side here, and secular liberals should not be afraid to invoke him. Policies of preemptive war and the upward redistribution of wealth are inversions of the Judeo-Christian ethic, which is for the most part silent, or mysteriously cryptic, on gays and abortion. At the very least, we need a firm commitment to public forms of child care, health care, housing, and education—for people of all faiths and no faith at all. Secondly, progressives should perhaps rethink their disdain for service-based outreach programs. Once it was the left that provided "alternative services" in the form of free clinics, women's health centers, food co-ops, and inner-city multiservice storefronts. Enterprises like these are not substitutes for an adequate public welfare state, but they can become the springboards from which to demand one.

One last lesson from the Christians—the ancient, original ones, that is. Theirs is the story of how a steadfast and heroic moral minority undermined the world's greatest empire and eventually came to power. Faced with relentless and spectacular forms of repression, they kept on meeting over their potluck dinners (the origins of later communion rituals), proselytizing and bearing witness wherever they could. Liberals and progressives need to emulate these original Christians, who stood against imperial Rome with their bodies, their hearts, and their souls.

Follies of Faith

AH, THE INGRATITUDE! WHEN PRESIDENT BUSH PRO-posed to redirect social spending through "faith-based" organizations, he must have been expecting the Christian right to burst into a chorus of hallelujahs at the prospect of being able to proselytize the wayward poor while doling out their food stamps and fuel oil vouchers. But no. Pat Robertson responded to the promised federal largesse by bitching and moaning about the possibility that it will go to the wrong sort of faith-based organization, such as, for example, the Hare Krishnas, the Scientologists, the Moonies, or the Nation of Islam. Some of these, he alleged, use "brainwashing techniques" and imagine that their leader is the messiah—frightful errors, of course, unless your religion happens to be Christianity.

And that's not the half of it. When Robertson dug into pagan imagery to describe Bush's faith-based initiative as a "Pandora's box," he forgot to mention the Hindus,

Buddhists, Sikhs, Jains, Wiccans; the adherents of Shinto, Santeria, and Voudun; or the members of peyote cults and followers of the Great Spirit, the Great Goddess, and Odin. All together, America boasts 1,350 "sects and denominations," a likely world record, even compared with the religiously promiscuous Roman Empire in the time of *Gladiator*. We may be the most religious of the industrialized nations—in terms of the proportion of the population that claims to believe in Unseen Beings and gathers regularly to commune with them—but we are also the most religiously disorganized, diverse, and confused.

This may be why the US lacks a uniform legal definition of "religion" that could be used to guide the distribution of faith-based charitable grants. A cursory scan of the relevant legal literature reveals that, to qualify as a religion for property tax exemptions, a group should (a) be incorporated and (b) claim a membership larger than a single nuclear family. It helps, too, if the group boasts accessories like "sacrament, ritual, [and] liturgy" and meets regularly for some purpose other than to discuss its progress toward achieving tax-exempt status. Nothing about size, though, or the content of those sacraments and rituals. Clearly anyone with imagination and legal counsel can start his or her own religion today and apply for funds from the Office of Faith-Based and Community Initiatives.

If you doubt your ability to come up with an entire new religion from scratch, and no Unseen Being has volunteered to dictate the instructions to you, there is plenty of more accessible help available. The Universal Life Church, for example, will ordain you for free, entirely by e-mail. Or, if you prefer your own church, check out Minister Charles Simpson, whose recent spam to Hotmail account holders announced his "power to make you a LEGALLY ORDAINED MINISTER within 48 hours!!!!" For a mere $29.95, you can "MARRY your BROTHER, SISTER, or your BEST FRIEND!! Don't settle for being the BEST MAN OR BRIDE'S MAID" and conduct funerals ("Don't settle for a minister you don't know!!"). Best of all, if you "WANT TO START YOUR OWN CHURCH," you can do so in a heartbeat, just as soon as you receive your certificate "IN COLOR, WITH GOLD SEAL," and "SHIPPING IS FREE!!!"

Why, though, limit yourself to inventing a new religion or church? In the debate over government support for religious institutions, the universal assumption has been that the term *faith-based organization* is coterminous with *religion*, but the *Encyclopedia Britannica* states firmly that "no definition allows for identification of 'faith' with 'religion.'" Scientology, for example, is one of the groups lining up for the new federal largesse. But what is an outfit that purports to teach the "science" of Dianetics doing in the "faith-based" category?

Scientology isn't the only faith-free "religion." Many well-known and respected religions, such as the Vedism of ancient India—or, in Luther's opinion, pre-Reformation Catholicism—have required little or no "faith." All you had to do was carry out the specified rituals—show up for the grand animal sacrifices (in the case of Vedism) or the mimed human sacrifice known as the mass (in the case of Catholicism). Nor, strictly speaking, should religions in which the relevant Unseen Beings actually and routinely manifest themselves be considered to be based on "faith." Followers of Voudun and Candomblé, for example, often experience "possession" by a deity; no "faith" or "belief" is necessary:

The Unseen Beings are a palpable fact of life, making these some of the world's rare *knowledge*-based religions.

Conversely, one can think of plenty of "faith-based" cults that would consider the label of "religion" an insult. Do you believe in the "historical mission of the proletariat" and "the inevitable triumph of socialism"? Do you get together regularly with friends who share these beliefs? Good, you and your pals clearly qualify as a "faith-based organization." Or perhaps you are a "market fundamentalist," holding that the capitalist market will—if given enough time and, of course, limitless freedom from regulation, trade barriers, etc.—uplift the downtrodden and solve all social ills. If market fundamentalism is a legitimate "faith," it may be that the privatization of welfare administrations to corporations like Lockheed and Maximus, initiated with Clinton's welfare reform, was an early experiment in the devolution of federal social programs to "faith-based organizations."

The real question, which so far not even the most ardent church-and-state separationists are raising is: why this odd privileging of faith over, say, knowledge or reason? Recall that *Webster's* offers as a general definition of faith "firm or unquestioning belief in something for which there is no proof." Would we want a faith-based defense system, for example, in which bombs are to be deflected by prayer? Or faith-based Medicare ("recite the rosary and call me in the morning")? The *New York Times* columnist Thomas Friedman has proposed, in a rare moment of levity, a faith-based system of air traffic control—although, truth be told, we already have that.

But the faith in faith-based institutions is no bar to paradox and contradiction: after all, the government order establishing faith-based charitable social services contains the inconsistent requirement that such projects be "results oriented," suggesting that they will be evaluated by Enlightenment methods involving empiricism and objective measurements. Still, don't let that deter you from applying for a grant for your personal religion's social service project: you can always assert, as a faith-based sort of person, that you truly *believe* it's working.

Pastors Go Postal

FOR ANYONE SEEKING AN EDIFYING TABLOID ALTERNA-tive to Britney and Lindsay or Jennifer and Angelina, August 2008 offered the civil trial of Victoria Osteen, wife of mega-church minister and televangelist Joel Osteen, for assaulting a flight attendant. The issue was what is sometimes described as a "spill" and sometimes as a "stain" on the armrest of Mrs. Osteen's first-class seat, which the flight attendant refused to clean up with sufficient alacrity because she was busy assisting others onboard. Although there is no evidence that the spill consisted of tuberculosis-ridden phlegm or avian flu–rich bird poop, Osteen was mightily pissed, allegedly pushing and punching the flight attendant and making such a ruckus that the Osteen family either left voluntarily or, depending on which side you believe, had to be removed from the flight.

I would be more sympathetic to the flight attendant, Sharon Brown, if she weren't demanding 10 percent of Osteen's fortune to compensate for injuries including a "loss of faith" and hemorrhoids somehow incurred from a frontal assault. But it isn't easy being a flight attendant in this era of layoffs, pay cuts, and packed planes—certainly not compared to being a millionaire on her way to Vail. Whatever dubious substance Victoria Osteen faced on that first-class armrest, she should have been able to derive some serenity from the fact that the church she co-pastors draws forty thousand worshippers a week and that her husband has been dubbed "America's Most Influential Christian."

Just another celebrity meltdown set off by insufficiently servile servers? Recall Russell Crowe's 2005 assault with a telephone on a SoHo hotel clerk, or Naomi Campbell's attacks with similar weapons—cell phone and Blackberry—on members of her own staff. But there's a curious antecedent here that Christians would do well to ponder: In 1997, another mega-church pastor and leading televangelist—Robert Schuller—was prosecuted for an eerily similar first-class tantrum.

Schuller, like the Osteens, is a proponent of positive thinking—the doctrine that God intends for you to be rich, healthy, and generally "great" right here in this life. While politicos have focused on the Christian Right, there's been far less attention to the fast growing brand of Christianity Lite, also represented by televangelists Joyce Meyer, Benny Hinn, and Creflo Dollar. Positive thinking is the theology of the modern mega-church, and it avoids all mention of sin—including the "sins" of abortion and homosexuality—lest such "negative" topics turn off any potential converts or "seekers." Like *The Secret*, it promises that you can have anything you want simply by "visualizing" it or, as Osteen puts it, "believing for it"—a doctrine derided by some Christian critics as "name it and claim it."

Schuller faced a different biohazard on his first-class

flight in '97—cheese. When the flight attendant gave him a fruit and cheese plate for dessert, Schuller insisted that the cheese be removed. The flight attendant refused, explaining, reasonably enough, that all the fruit had been plated with cheese and could be contaminated, from a cheese-allergy sufferer's point of view. But the pastor was simply on a low-fat diet and did not want to see the cheese on his plate, so he got out of his seat and accosted the flight attendant, shaking him violently by the shoulders. Schuller ended up paying an $1,100 fine and was placed under supervision by a federal agent for six months.

In the theology of Christian positive thinking, "everything happens for a reason." The Osteens may conclude that the divine intention was to prod them into emulating Joyce Meyers and Creflo Dollar by investing in a private jet. But there's another possible message from on high—that this brand of Christianity fosters a distinctly un-Christian narcissism.

Consider the ways the Lord works in the life of the Osteens, as recounted in Joel's book *Your Best Life Now*, which has sold four million copies and is graced by a back cover photo of the smiling couple. Acting through Victoria, who kept "speaking words of faith and victory" on the subject, Joel was led to build the family "an elegant home." On other occasions, God intervened to save Joel from a speeding ticket and to get him not only a good parking spot but "the premier spot in that parking lot." Why God did not swoop down with a sponge and clean up the offending stain on the armrest remains a mystery, because Osteen's deity is less the Master of the Universe than an obliging factotum.

Plenty of Christians have already made the point that the positive thinking of Christianity Lite is demeaning to God, and I leave them to pursue this critique. More importantly, from a secular point of view, it's dismissive of other humans, and not only flight attendants. If a person is speeding, shouldn't he get a ticket to deter him from endangering others? And if Osteen gets the premier parking spot, what about all the other people consigned to the remote fringes of the lot? Christianity, at best, is about a sacrificial love for others, not about getting to the head of the line.

If the Osteens' brand of religion is what flight attendant Sharon Brown lost faith in as a result of being manhandled on that plane to Vail, then the suit should have been dropped, because Victoria Osteen had already done her enough of a favor. The jury must have agreed with me because it found in Osteen's favor.

Is It Safe to Go
Back to Church?

WHAT IS THIS STRANGE FRAGRANCE IN THE AIR? Could it be Christian spirit? The President of the Christian Coalition is calling on his coreligionists to make environmental protection a foremost consideration in their election choices. In early 2006, eighty-six evangelical leaders signed a statement calling for action on global warming. In the UK, evangelicals are spearheading a campaign to "Make Poverty History." It seems like only yesterday that right-winger and self-professed evangelical Dick Armey criticized Republicans for "talking about things like gay marriage and so forth," while the Democrats were "talking about things people care about, like how do I pay my bills?" Could it be that the erstwhile Christian right has found Jesus?

It's possible that the Republicans' most reliable trick–*distraction*–is beginning to wear thin. Distraction was the means to get people to vote against their own economic self-interest–that is, for tax cuts for the rich, cuts in social programs for everyone else, and endless war. The *real* threats to well-being, people were told, are abortionists, stem cell researchers, and matrimonially minded gays.

With a lot of help from the megachurches, the Republicans pulled off the trick for years. All the guy in the pulpit had to say was "vote pro-life" or "save the family from marauding gays," and the message got through: vote Republican, which translated into feed the fat cats straight from your wallet.

But as someone once said, you can't fool all the people every single moment. It's hard to continue getting bent out of shape about the fate of a zygote or embryonic stem cell when you can't afford to take your sick three-year-old to a doctor. It makes no sense to blame gays for the strains that arise in your marriage where one partner has to work days and the other nights because you can't afford child care. And it's a stretch to put your faith in gay-bashing Republican politicos when so many of their own family members and staffers are contently gay.

This doesn't mean that morals and values have no place in politics. On the contrary, what everyone needs to understand is that economic issues *are* moral issues. Poverty is a moral issue; 47 million Americans without health insurance is a moral issue. The same goes for the environment: why fight to save a fertilized egg cell for a life spent gasping for air or fleeing the ever-rising coastlines? If you're going to be prolife, you've got to be proenvironment and pro–economic justice.

As for the doctrinal part of the Christian right's agenda: show me the passage in the Bible that bans stem cell research. See if you can find the tiniest allusion to abortion. Yes, there's homophobia in the Bible, along with endorsements of slavery and a weird obsession with animal sacrifice. Not a word, it should be mentioned, about gay marriage.

Poverty and economic injustice, on the other hand, get over three thousand hits in the Bible. Left-wing evangelist Jim Wallis once took scissors to a Bible and cut out all the references to economic injustice—and what was left looked a lot like confetti. Jesus was a hard-liner on the redistribution of wealth: remember what he told the rich man who wanted to get into heaven? Imagine what he'd have to say about the Bush tax cuts.

So welcome back to the fold, all you recovering right-wing evangelists! We'll still have plenty to argue about: I'm prochoice, pro–stem cell research, and against anyone getting married when some people aren't allowed to. But at least we may have enough common ground on which to hold a meaningful debate.

God Owes Us an Apology

THE TSUNAMI OF SEA WATER THAT HIT SOUTH ASIA WAS followed instantly by a tsunami of spittle as the religious sputtered to rationalize God's latest felony. Here we'd been, placidly killing one another a few dozen at a time in Iraq, Darfur, Congo, Israel, and Palestine, when along comes the deity and whacks a quarter million in a couple of hours between breakfast and lunch. On CNN, NPR, and Fox News and in newspaper articles too numerous for Nexis to count, men and women of the cloth weighed in solemnly on His existence, His motives, and even His competence to continue as Ruler of Everything.

Theodicy, in other words—the attempt to reconcile God's perfect goodness with the manifest evils of His world—has arisen from the waves. On the retro, fundamentalist side, various clergymen of the cloth announced that the tsunami was the rational act of a deity enraged by (take your pick): the suppression of Christianity in South Asia, pornography and child trafficking in that same locale, or, in the view of some Muslim commentators, the bikini-clad tourists at Phuket.

On the more liberal end of the theological spectrum, God's spokespeople hastened to stuff their fingers in the dike even as the floodwaters of doubt washed over it. Of course God exists seems to be the general consensus. And of course He is perfectly good. It's just that His jurisdiction doesn't extend to tectonic plates. Or maybe it does and He tosses us an occasional grenade like this just to see how quickly we can mobilize to clean up the damage. Besides, as the Catholic priests like to remind us, "He's a 'mystery,'"– though that's never stopped them from pronouncing His views on abortion with absolute certainty.

The clerics who struggled to make sense of the tsunami must not have noticed that this was hardly the first display of God's penchant for wanton, homicidal mischief. Leaving out man-made genocide, war, and even those "natural" disasters, like drought and famine, to which "man" invariably contributes through His inept social arrangements, God has a lot to account for in the way of earthquakes, hurricanes, tornadoes, and plagues. Nor has He ever shown much discrimination in His choice of victims. A tsunami hit Lisbon in 1755, on All Saints' Day, when the good Christians were in church. The faithful perished, while the denizens of the red light district, which was built on strong stone, simply carried on sinning. Similarly, when hurricanes flattened the God-fearing, Republican parts of Florida in 2004, sin-soaked Key West and South Beach were spared.

The Christian-style "God of love" should be particularly vulnerable to post-tsunami doubts. What kind of "love" inspired Him to wrest babies from their parents' arms, the better to drown them in a hurry? If He so loves us that He gave His only son, etc., why couldn't He have held those tectonic plates in place at least until the kids were off the beach? So much, too, for the current pop-Christian God, who can be found, at least on the Internet, micromanaging people's careers, resolving marital spats, and taking excess pounds off the faithful—this last being one of Pat Robertson's recent fixations.

If we are responsible for our actions, as most religions insist, then God should be too, and I would propose, post-tsunami, an immediate withdrawal of prayer and other forms of flattery directed at a supposedly moral deity—at least until an apology is issued, like, for example: "I was so busy with Cindy in Omaha's weight-loss program that I wasn't paying attention to the earth's crust."

It's not just Christianity. Any religion centered on a God who is both all-powerful and all-good, including Islam and the more monotheistically inclined versions of Hinduism, should be subject to a thorough post-tsunami evaluation. As many have noted before me: if God cares about our puny species, then disasters prove that He is not all-powerful; and if He *is* all-powerful, then clearly He doesn't give a damn.

In fact, the best way for the religious to fend off the atheist threat might be to revive the old bad, or at least amoral and indifferent, gods. The tortured notion of a God who is both good and powerful is fairly recent, dating to roughly 1200 BC, after which Judaism, Christianity, Buddhism, and Islam emerged. Before that, you had the feckless Greco-Roman pantheon, whose members interfered in human events only when their considerable egos were at stake. Or you had monstrous, human-sacrifice-consuming, psycho-gods like Ba'al and his Central American counterparts. Even earlier, there were prehistoric gods and goddesses modeled on man-eating animals like lions and requiring a steady diet of human or animal sacrificial flesh.

The faithful will protest that they don't want to worship a bad or amoral or indifferent god, but obviously they already do. Why not acknowledge what our prehistoric ancestors knew? If the Big Guy or Gal operates in any kind of moral framework, it has nothing to do with the rules we've come up with over the eons as primates attempting to live in groups—rules like, for example, "no hitting."

Yes, the tsunami was a warning, though not about the hazards of wearing bikinis. What it comes down to is that we're up shit creek here on the planet Earth. We're wide open to asteroid hits—in the latest near miss a city-sized one passed within a mere million miles of Earth. Then, too, it's only a matter of time before the constant shuffling of viral DNA results in a global pandemic. And the tsunami was a reminder that the planet itself is a jerry-rigged affair, likely to keep belching and lurching. Even leaving out global warming and the possibility of nuclear war, this is not a good situation, in case you hadn't yet noticed.

If there is a God and He, She, or It had a message for us as the waters rushed in, that message is: Get your act together, folks—your seismic detection systems, your first responders, and your global mobilization capacity. The fact is no one, and I do mean no One, is coming to medevac us out of here.

Postscript: Rich Get Poorer, Poor Disappear

AFTER YEARS OF CHRONICLING PLUNDER AND EXPLOITA-
tion, misery and greed, I am tempted to delete "class
inequality" from my worry list. Less than a year ago, it was
the biggest economic threat on the horizon, with even hard-
line conservative pundits grousing that wealth was flowing
uphill at an alarming rate, leaving the middle class stuck
with stagnating incomes while the new superrich ascended
to the heavens in their personal jets. Then the whole top-
heavy structure of American capitalism began to totter,
and—poof!—inequality all but vanished from the public discourse. A financial columnist in the *Chicago Sun-Times* just
announced that the recession is a "great leveler," serving to
"democratize the agony," as we all tumble into "the Nouveau Poor."

The media have been pelting us with heart-wrenching
stories about the neo-suffering of the Nouveau Poor, or at
least the Formerly Superrich among them: Foreclosures in
Greenwich, Connecticut! A collapsing market for cosmetic

surgery! Sales of Gulfstream jets declining! Nieman Marcus and Saks Fifth Avenue on the ropes! We read of desperate measures, like having to cut back the personal trainer to two hours a week. Parties have been canceled; dinner guests have been offered, gasp, baked potatoes and chili. The *New York Times* relates the story of a New Jersey teenager whose parents were forced to cut her one-hundred-dollars-a-week allowance and private Pilates classes. In one of the most pathetic tales of all, New Yorker Alexandra Penney relates how she lost her life savings to Bernie Madoff and is now faced with having to lay off her three-day-a-week maid, Yolanda. "I wear a classic clean white shirt every day of the week. I have about forty white shirts. They make me feel fresh and ready to face whatever battles I may be fighting ..." she wrote, but without Yolanda, "How am I going to iron those shirts so I can still feel like a poor civilized person?"

But hard times are no more likely to abolish class inequality than Obama's inauguration is likely to eradicate racism. No one actually knows yet whether inequality has increased or decreased during this last year of recession, but the historical precedents are not promising. The economists I've talked to—like Joe Biden's top economic advisor, Jared Bernstein—insist that recessions are particularly unkind to the poor and the middle class. Canadian economist Armine Yalnizyan says, "Income polarization always gets worse during recessions." It makes sense. If the stock market has shrunk your assets of $500 million to a mere $250 million, you may have to pass on a third or fourth vacation home. But if you've just lost an $8-an-hour job, you're looking at no home at all.

All right, I'm a journalist and I understand how the media work. When a millionaire cuts back on his crème fraîche and caviar consumption, you have a touching human interest story. But pitch a story about a laid-off roofer who loses his trailer home and you're likely to get a big editorial yawn. "Poor Get Poorer" is just not an eye-grabbing headline, even when the evidence is overwhelming. Food stamp applications, for example, are rising toward a historic record; calls to one D.C.-area hunger hotline have jumped 248 percent in the last six months, most of them from people who have never needed food aid before. And for the first time since 1996, there's been a marked upswing in the number of people seeking cash assistance from TANF (Temporary Aid to Needy Families), the exsanguinated version of welfare left by welfare "reform." Too bad for them that TANF is essentially a wage-supplement program based on the assumption that the poor would always be able to find jobs, and that it pays, at most, less than half the federal poverty level.

Why do the sufferings of the poor and the downwardly mobile class matter more than the tiny deprivations of the rich? Leaving aside all the softhearted socialist, Christian-type arguments, it's because poverty and the squeeze on the middle class are a big part of what got us into this mess in the first place. Only one thing kept the sub-rich spending in the oo's, and hence kept the economy going, and that was debt: credit card debt, home equity loans, car loans, college loans and of course the now famously "toxic" subprime mortgages, which were bundled and sliced into "securities" and marketed to the rich as high-interest investments throughout the world. The gross inequality of American society wasn't just unfair or aesthetically displeasing; it created a perilously unstable situation.

Which is why any serious government attempt to get the economy going again—and I leave aside the unserious attempts like bank bailouts and other corporate-welfare projects—has to address the grievous issue of inequality. Obama is promising to generate three million new jobs in "shovel ready" projects, and let's hope they're not all jobs for young men with strong backs. Until those jobs kick in, and in case they leave out the elderly, the single moms, and the downsized desk-workers, we're going to need an economic policy centered on the poor: more money for food stamps, for Medicaid, unemployment insurance, and, yes, cash assistance along the lines of what welfare once was, so that when people come tumbling down they don't end up six feet under. For those who think "welfare" sounds too radical, we could just call it a "right to life" program, only one in which the objects of concern have already been born.

If that sounds politically unfeasible, consider this: When Clinton was cutting welfare and food stamps in the '90s, the poor were still an easily marginalized group, subjected to the nastiest sorts of racial and gender stereotyping. They were lazy, promiscuous, addicted deadbeats, as whole choruses of conservative experts announced. Thanks to the recession, however—and I knew there had to be a bright side—the ranks of the poor are swelling every day with failed business-owners, office workers, salespeople, and long-time homeowners. Stereotype that! As the poor and the formerly middle class Nouveau Poor become the American majority, they will finally have the clout to get their needs met.

Acknowledgments

Thanks to Diane Alexander, Riva Hocherman—and, as always, my brilliant editor Sara Bershtel—for their help in compiling this book.

Thanks as well to the following publications, where versions of some of these pieces previously appeared: *Los Angeles Times* ("Got Grease?", "A Society That Throws the Sick Away"), *The New York Times* ("Who Moved My Ability to Reason?", "All Together Now," "A Uterus Is Not a Substitute for a Conscience," "Let Them Eat Wedding Cake," "Owning Up to Abortion," "The New Cosby Kids"), *The Progressive* ("Class Struggle 101," "The Cheapskate Warfare State," "Follies of Faith," "God Owes Us an Apology") and *The Nation* ("The Faith Factor").

ABOUT THE AUTHOR

BARBARA EHRENREICH is the author of fifteen books, including *Dancing in the Streets* and the *New York Times* bestsellers *Nickel and Dimed* and *Bait and Switch*. A frequent contributor to *Harper's* and *The Nation*, she has also been a columnist at *The New York Times* and *Time* magazine.

She can be reached at www.barbaraehrenreich.com.